Uninvested

Uninvested

HOW WALL STREET
HIJACKS YOUR MONEY
AND HOW TO FIGHT BACK

BOBBY MONKS

with
JUSTIN JAFFE and BREE LACASSE

PORTFOLIO / PENGUIN

PORTFOLIO / PENGUIN
An imprint of Penguin Random House LLC
375 Hudson Street
New York, New York 10014
penguin.com

Illustrations on pages xxii, 37, 43, 104, 108, 136: Aaron Staples
Illustrations on pages 3, 72, 87, 116: Kristen Schwenger

ISBN: 978-1-59184-819-6
Printed in the United States of America

1   3   5   7   9   10   8   6   4   2

Set in Life LT Std
Designed by Jaime Putorti

For Willard Libby

Sleepwalking, contrary to most belief, apparently has little to do with dreaming. In fact, it occurs when the sleeper is enjoying his most oblivious, deepest sleep . . .

—"Sleepwalker Not Dreaming,"
SCIENCE NEWS, JUNE 25, 1966

Contents

Preface

I.

We, the investors, have fallen asleep.

Sure, we occasionally wake up to glance at our portfolios. We look at our zigging and zagging account balances. We file—or, more likely, recycle—our monthly statements. Our investments grow or wither.

But there's really nothing for us to do about it. So, back to sleep.

Sometimes our sleep is disrupted by uneasy dreams or nagging doubts. How exactly does this whole investment system work? Why did we buy that mutual fund? What caused our account balance to go up or down? What happens to the money we invest?

We toss and turn, uncertain of who is managing our money. We hope our financial adviser is the omniscient captain, expertly navigating ever-shifting market currents. But perhaps our portfolios are simply bobbing along the surface of the Dow Jones Industrial Average, ascending when the tide rises and sinking as it retreats.

On occasion, we are gripped by nightmares. We fear our own money has been turned against us, invested in companies we deplore. We worry that our capital has made us complicit, endowing the perpetrators of environmental ruin, financial apocalypse, and political dysfunction.

There is just so much we don't know as we sleep.

We are only one generation removed from a financial world that was far simpler, more transparent, and less risky than the one we live in now. But the landscape for investors continues to evolve into one that's more complex, opaque, and speculative. And we grow ever more dependent on financial instruments that are a mystery to us and on money managers whose incentives are obscure.

We lie with our eyes closed now, deep in our reverie, but with a dawning awareness that the sheep we are counting are being fleeced. And that they are us.

II.
—

Financial firms and money managers have intentionally made investing overly complicated and then convinced us that we cannot do it on our own. They have elbowed their way into every corner of investing, cultivating a financial intermediary complex that disconnects us from our capital and charges us handsomely for it.

Money managers control trillions of investors' dollars, which makes them highly influential in social, environmental, financial, and political matters. As we have seen after two scandal-driven recessions, their strategy has been to leverage this influence primarily to advance their own interests.

Having interacted with the financial sector throughout nearly every phase of my career, I was not surprised to learn of the ethically dubious activity that led to the most recent economic downturn in 2008. Though many well-intentioned financial advisers and money managers serve their clients with integrity, unscrupulous activity has long been pervasive in this industry, though it has been due to systemic deficiencies as much as the behavior of bad actors. What did surprise me, however, was the passivity of investors.

Even in the decades preceding the most recent downturn, very few investors enjoyed financial success equal to that of their money managers. Given this, I have long wondered why investors don't pull their money out of the system en masse.

I suspect that it is because most feel powerless. Unaware of the implications of their investments and unable to penetrate the excruciating complexity of the system that facilitates them, many seek refuge in their money managers' aura of sophistication, pretense of competence, and projection of certainty. It seems to me that most investors are simply sleepwalking through the investing process.

They have become uninvested.

III.

Discomfited by the increasing dysfunction I've observed in the financial sector over the past thirty years, I decided to help investors break out of this unhappy dream state and reinvest in themselves as owners. As a serial entrepreneur whose ventures have included building, buying, and running companies involved in banking and investment services as well as real estate development, media, and technology, I figured I could offer insights from my experience working in and around the financial sector—both as executive and customer, investor and creditor, and almost always as an active, awake, and engaged participant.

I started my career by developing real estate projects, which gave me my first taste of dealing with banks and investors as well as an array of state and government regulators.

Later, I was a cofounder and served as chairman of the executive committee of Atlantic Bank and Trust. I oversaw activities ranging from capital formation to derivatives to government regulation, and observed firsthand the importance of communication, trust, and transparency in managing other people's money.

I was the chairman of Institutional Shareholder Services and of Proxy Monitor, the two largest global proxy voting services. I worked on the front lines of corporate governance issues, including disclosure and executive compensation, and witnessed the power of organized shareholders in enforcing accountability in corporations.

I am an owner of Mediant Communications, which facilitates shareholder communication. This position has enhanced my understanding of the complexity of corporate disclosure and the inherent challenges in giving investors accurate, timely, comprehensible information.

Until recently, I was chairman of Spinnaker Trust, a company that has more than $1 billion under management. This gave me a ringside view of the inadequacies of modern money management. I am also an owner and director of iiWisdom, a startup dedicated to improving communication between institutional investors and their portfolio companies in order to increase accountability.

In 2010, I began to study the financial sector more formally, paying particular attention to the relationship between investors and money managers. I partnered with two researchers, Bree LaCasse and Justin Jaffe, to investigate the mechanics of this sector and its unique role in the economy, hoping to figure out how to counteract its unsustainable trajectory.

We are not academics nor are we traditional journalists, though we drew on the excellent and rigorous work of both in writing this book. We spent hundreds of hours researching, reading, and conducting interviews with knowledgeable figures such as Jack Bogle, founder of the Vanguard Group, one of the largest investment management companies in the world, legendary activist investor Carl Icahn, and former congressman and financial reformer Barney Frank, coauthor of the landmark Dodd-Frank Wall Street Reform and Consumer Protection Act.

We spoke with dozens of industry insiders in order to gather a wide array of informed insights from a variety of perspectives. We investigated the solutions offered by legislators, regulators, accountants, credit-rating agencies, journalists, and other traditional agents of accountability.

To learn how the financial sector got its hands on so much of our money, we examined the changing nature of retirement saving and how it came to drive such a huge share of investment activity. We explored how the vaunted mutual fund came to dominate the landscape through the individual retirement arrangement (IRA) and the 401(k). I also incorporated my own experiences with investing in private equity and hedge funds as well as mainstream products like mutual funds. Some of these entities have invested in my business ventures. Despite the real and major differences among them, I have found that a similar set of problems undermines them all. Indeed, regardless of the point of entry, investors' capital ends up in a monolithic financial system that plays by an asymmetric and nebulous set of rules.

We sleep at our own peril.

IV.

Continuing to invest somnolently in this flawed system endangers our own personal portfolios—but also our environment, economy, political system, and society. In outsourcing our investments, whether to a money manager or mutual fund, we sacrifice control—but not responsibility.

In writing this book, our goals are to share what we have learned and to convince you that the best (and only) way to fix this broken system is to awaken a critical mass of engaged investors.

With a group of partners, I am also exploring a new kind of money management model, a *cooperative investment partnership*, that puts the customer back in control and makes investing more ethical and profitable for investors.

We want to empower investors by enhancing their understanding of what really happens with their capital. We want to restore their sense of ownership. And we want to increase their proximity to the benefits and responsibilities of investing.

We want to help them become reinvested.

Investors and money managers must share the risks, costs, benefits, and responsibilities of the investments they make together. If we can rebalance the relationship, we can fix many of the most significant problems facing our society, environment, and economy.

Robert C. S. Monks

Portland, Maine

January 2015

Uninvested

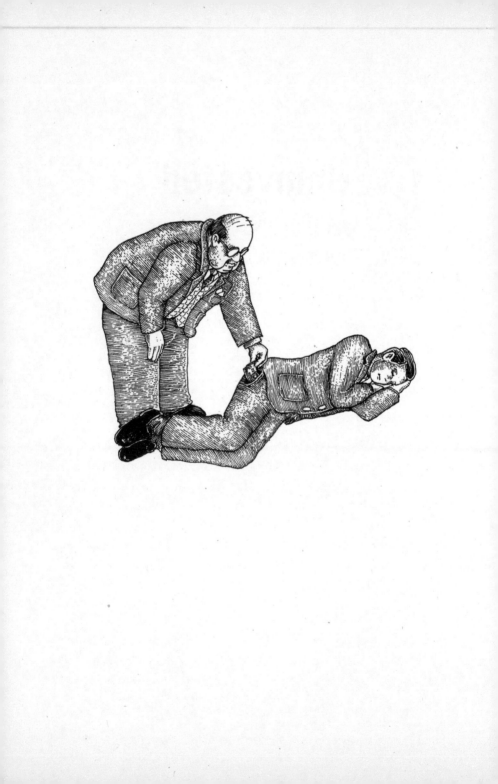

1

An Investor's Dream:
Ownership Outsourced

For much of the twentieth century, financial institutions focused mostly on taking deposits and lending cash and credit to people and businesses. The finance industry overall was far more low-key and nondescript than it is today. This is one reason *Mad Men*, set in the 1960s, focuses on an advertising agency and not a bank.

In 1952, with the Great Depression still fresh in the nation's collective memory, less than 5 percent of the US population owned stocks.[1] And until the 1970s, most middle-class Americans' financial activities were relatively simple, transparent, and low risk: a checking or savings account, a thirty-year mortgage, a small business loan transacted with a local bank.

Even without a background in finance, most people could comprehend the economic terms and implications of these arrangements. And in most cases, they had personal relationships with the financial professionals with whom they were doing business.

Though the seeds of social and political turbulence were being sown in the 1950s, it was a simpler era financially. No massive, international banking conglomerates. No high-speed trading. No credit default swaps. Fewer "professionals" were peddling advice. It was a time when it was considered reasonable for regular people to manage their own investing.

One such regular investor was Willard Libby, the father of a longtime friend. I had heard over the years many stories about Willard and his skepticism about the financial industry. He sounded like a kindred spirit.

As I began to work on this book, I knew that I would want to talk to Willard.

So I did.

Willard's Story

Born in 1915 in Waterville, Maine, Willard Dunn Libby was the son of Mabel Esther Dunn Libby and Dr. Herbert Carlyle Libby, a professor at Colby College. Willard was educated at the Coburn Classical Institute and Colby College (class of 1937). After a year of postgraduate study in chemistry at MIT, he took a summer job in 1938 that turned into a forty-year career with Eastman Kodak. When war broke out in 1941, he was assigned to work on a government project, which exempted him from the draft. Rather than stay behind, however, Willard circumnavigated the regulations and enlisted in the US Navy, serving in the Pacific. He was stationed in Okinawa at the end of war.

Willard Dunn Libby

On his way to fight in the Pacific, Willard met the woman who would become his wife, Rebecca Marshall Stribling. Like Willard, she was serving in the navy. As she had been commissioned before him, she outranked him, which he pointed out whenever the subject arose thereafter. After they married, Willard and Rebecca lived in Rochester, New York, in a modest apartment, until they had saved enough money to take out a small mortgage. They bought land on a bluff overlooking the Irondequoit Bay.

After five years, they had paid off the mortgage and had two kids. Willard raced his sailboat on the bay during the summers, and in the winters he skied or built electronics or did carpentry in the shop in the basement. He got up early in the snowy winters to plow the driveway before he went to work. The cars he drove were bottom-of-the-line Chevrolets or Fords, and he always paid cash for them.

Willard read the *Wall Street Journal* daily and wrote personal letters to senators and presidents. He had no formal financial education aside from what he picked up during a stint as a member of an investing club when he was in his twenties. Willard was not a self-taught financial whiz nor someone obsessed about his investments. Still, he felt confident in his capacity to manage his portfolio. And his strategy was simple and consistent: buy stock in a few companies that he believed in, and hold it for the long term.

Throughout his life, Willard paid attention to his investments. He read the newspaper. He watched the news. He did his homework. He wasn't obsessed or fixated on the market, but he took his responsibility as an investor seriously.

This strategy paid off. Throughout his life, Willard supported the companies in which he invested. And as his portfolio grew in value, these companies supported him, too, allowing him to live comfortably and independently until he died in 2014.

The End of an Era

During Willard's lifetime, mainstream Americans' financial practices underwent major transformations. One of the big factors in this was the shift in responsibility for retirement saving from traditional employer pensions to employee retirement accounts and 401(k)s. Driven by a host of economic, regulatory, and demographic tailwinds, this shift opened the door for financial corporations and money managers to offer a new class of products and solutions to help middle-class Americans invest their savings to fund their retirements.

Spurred by new tax incentives associated with these investments, and with fewer opportunities to lean on traditional employer-provided pensions, Americans quickly moved a massive amount of wealth into these new investment vehicles. The crown jewel of them, the mutual fund, drew billions of dollars of Americans' assets and, in turn, invested them in stocks and other market-based securities. By 1990, more than 25 percent of US households owned mutual funds (see Figure 1).

The "financialization" of America had begun.

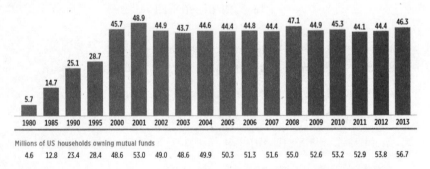

Millions of US households owning mutual funds
4.6 12.8 23.4 28.4 48.6 53.0 49.0 48.6 49.9 50.3 51.3 51.6 55.0 52.6 53.2 52.9 53.8 56.7

Source: Investment Company Institute and US Census Bureau

Figure 1. Percentage of US Households
Owning Mutual Funds, 1980–2013

By 2007, roughly two-thirds of all adults in the United States had money in the market,[2] and the vast majority of them relied on "professionals" to manage their investments. Though some people still bought stocks, bonds, and other securities themselves, most invested through a 401(k), individual retirement arrangement (IRA), or mutual fund. Even though the Great Recession sent many running for the exits, the majority of Americans remain in the market today, and a massive industry of financial advisers and money managers has evolved to meet their perceived needs (see Figure 2).

Do you, personally, or jointly with a spouse, have any money invested in the stock market right now—either in an individual stock, a stock mutual fund, or in a self-directed 401(k) or IRA?

■ % Yes   ▨ % No

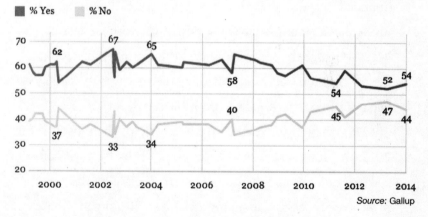

Source: Gallup

Figure 2. Percentage of US Adults Invested in the Stock Market

Tough Times Test a Relationship

In October 2008, at the zenith of American participation in the stock market, the economy imploded in a subprime mortgage–driven catastrophe. Roughly $1 trillion of invested capital evaporated. According to labor economist Teresa Ghilarducci, "Everybody overnight who had a 401(k) or an IRA saw their accounts drop by 25 percent on average. But many people saw their accounts drop by half. The 401(k) in October of 2008 had become a 201(k)."[3]

Very few had any understanding of what had happened, why it had happened, or who had caused it.

One thing that was clear, though, was that most of the financial corporations and money managers handling our investments emerged from the downturn with far less collateral damage than the rest of us—this despite the fact that the postmortem reporting has proved that it was their risky behavior that was largely responsible for the crisis.

Though many investors are still recouping their losses in 2015, the downturn was brief for most of the largest financial corporations and their top brass. In 2009, after the worst American recession in many decades,[4] JPMorgan Chase earned nearly $12 billion in profits on record revenue of

$108.6 billion;[5] CEO Jamie Dimon took home more than $16 million in salary and bonus.[6] Bank of America reported nearly $121 billion in revenue and $6.3 billion in net income.[7] The bank's CEO, Ken Lewis, who left in 2009, took no annual salary for the year but collected $53 million in pension benefits and $11 million in deferred compensation on his way out the door.[8] Wells Fargo reported revenue of $89 billion and net income of $12.3 billion,[9] paving the way for CEO John G. Stumpf to pocket more than $21 million.[10]

Meanwhile, median household income in the United States continues to stagnate,[11] and was lower in 2013 than it was in 1999 (see Figure 3).

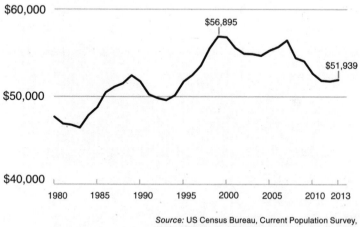

Source: US Census Bureau, Current Population Survey, 1968 to 2014 Annual Social and Economic Supplements

Figure 3. US Median Household Income, 1980–2013

One of the incontrovertible lessons of this experience is that the market's vicissitudes don't apply to financial corporations and money managers. They consistently rake in colossal profits to pay executives' formidable salaries whether or not they actually earn returns for investors.

In fact, the financial sector's profits have never been higher, and they now account for roughly one-third of total US corporate profits annually (see Figure 4).[12] Regardless

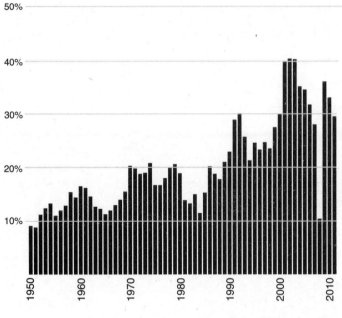

Source: Bureau of Economic Analysis

Figure 4. Financial Sector Profits as a Percentage of
Total Domestic Corporate Profits, 1950–2011

of portfolio size, asset class, or market focus, many investors' returns (or lack thereof) have little or no connection to their money managers' compensation.

An Unequal Partnership

Mutuality has been drained from the modern investor–money manager relationship. As the percentage of the population investing has increased, investors' understanding of and active participation in the process has dwindled. Though investors have put trillions of dollars into this system, there is widespread confusion about what actually happens to the money once it's there.

One thing that is apparent, however, is that investors have largely been cut out of the action, disenfranchised from their capital. "Hand over your money," our financial advisers and money managers have said, "and we'll take care of the rest."

And hand it over we have. In 1950, individual investors directly owned 93 percent of US public equities;[13] in 2010, financial intermediaries controlled roughly 75 percent of US equities and more than $37 trillion in securities (see Figure 5).[14]

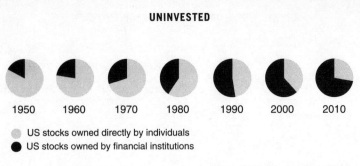

Source: Federal Reserve Flow of Funds

Figure 5. Share of Ownership of US Equities by Individual Investors and Financial Intermediaries, 1950–2010

But some investors are tiring of standing on the sidelines.

We have examined this complicated, asymmetrical relationship between investors and money managers, and explored the system that facilitates these unequal relationships. We have studied the system and the incentives that shape it. We have rooted out the major factors that have bred this inequality and the misunderstanding, suspicion, and animosity that it engenders between investors and money managers.

We have learned there is a common set of issues plaguing nearly every class of investment in every corner of the financial industry. Whether you're in a mutual fund, exchange-traded fund (ETF), real estate investment trust, hedge fund, private equity fund, or any other collective investment scheme, you are likely to run up against one or more of the major problems we've identified.

Modern Finance: Nine Universal Problems

1. Broken English. If you've attempted to read a mutual fund prospectus or quarterly statement, you're acquainted with the financial industry's knack for bewildering investors with dense technical, financial, and legal jargon.

2. Suspect Advice. When you walk into a Fidelity branch or "talk to Chuck," the person you are most likely to meet is a financial salesperson. Most of these "advisers" serve one master—the big-box corporation that pays them to sell its most profitable products. This conflict of interest ultimately taints almost everything they do.

3. Size Matters. The sheer scale of most collective investment products makes it hard for investors to know what they actually own. The most popular modern investment, the mutual fund, invests in hundreds of corporations simultaneously. As a result, most shareholders have no idea where their capital ends up.

4. Different Values. Collective investment products make investors vulnerable to unknowingly supporting companies they may not like. In fact, your mutual fund may be funneling your money into corporations you despise.

5. Enigmatic Fees. Given the challenges financial firms have in communicating clearly and comprehensively, most investors lack a full understanding of the fees they pay for their investments.

6. Always Paid. Whether investors realize it or not, most money managers collect fees whether or not they generate returns for clients. Those fees feed executives' salaries whether or not they've done anything to deserve them.

7. Not Invested. Few money managers disclose to clients whether—or how much—they have personally invested in the products and services they sell. We should all be wary of chefs who don't eat their own cooking.

8. Zero Accountability. In an industry that's far less concerned with generating returns than collecting fees, there's little incentive to enforce accountability internally or externally.

9. Dirty Data. Most money managers base their investment decisions on unreliable information sources, such as accounting statements and conventional credit ratings that are paid for by the very companies they profess to examine.

Trapped in the
Financial Intermediary Complex

As of 2010, financial institutions and money managers controlled more than 75 percent of all US equities and $37 trillion in securities.[15] That's more than half of the financial assets of US households.[16] More than half of all the money we have—much of it wrapped up in 401(k)s and IRAs and mutual funds and pension funds—is ultimately in their hands.

Regardless of your point of entry into the financial system, whether through a 401(k) or individual retirement account, a mutual fund or ETF, a hedge fund or pension fund, you inevitably end up feeding a monolithic financial intermediary complex whose primary, and sometimes sole, objective is making money for its highest-paid executives.

Exerting its power through aggressive marketing, persistent lobbying, and raw financial prowess, the money management industry has relieved most investors of the benefits and responsibilities of ownership. In outsourcing our investing to corporations with whom we have little direct contact or communication, we have also given up much of our ability to hold them responsible for their failure to perform or represent our interests. And they know it.

There's a domino effect: without empowered investors capable of holding money managers accountable, there's little incentive for money managers to hold corporate managers at their portfolio companies accountable. This lack of accountability has allowed our most intractable problems to go largely unattended—from unsustainable foresting practices to toxic spills to the widening gap between CEO (chief executive officer) compensation and average worker salaries.

What happened? Why haven't we risen up to demand a change? Why have we allowed this industry to take control of our money and use it so irresponsibly? At the bare minimum, why haven't we pulled our capital out of this broken system?

One factor is the ubiquity of the industry's most profitable products and services: 401(k) plans, IRAs, and especially mutual funds. These have become the central mechanisms for retirement saving and investment for middle-class Americans. Government-sponsored tax incentives have increased their appeal. Conventional wisdom has it that putting money into a mutual fund is a smart and responsible way to invest.

Another reason is that many investors feel utterly powerless. We feel too busy, under-informed, and overwhelmed to manage our own investments. We have been numbed by the intentional complexity of the system that facilitates our investing. We have excused ourselves from the table, unwilling or incapable of addressing our own financial reality.

Simultaneously, we feel reassured by our money managers' "expertise," comforted by their impeccable academic credentials, nice suits, and supreme confidence. They talk a good game, and seem to know more than we do. So we give them our money. This illusion of omniscience and omnipotence has given financial professionals a license to co-opt our capital and harvest it for their own purposes.

In addition, many of the safeguards we've relied on to keep the system balanced, and to keep financial firms accountable, have been neutralized. The Enron scandal and the crisis in mortgage-backed securities exposed the impotence of conventional accounting, auditing, and credit-rating practices. Other traditional watchdogs such as government agencies and investigative journalists are less equipped than ever to take on a financial sector with superior power, resources, and influence.

We, too, are to blame. When times were good, we were happy. When you're getting a stupendous return, a 2 percent fee doesn't sound terrible. Outsourcing our investing, however, even when we profit, makes us partners with the corporations and securities in which our money is invested, whether we realize it or not.

For most Americans, investing has become a complex, speculative, and ultimately inscrutable enterprise. Awash in credit default swaps, collateralized debt obligations, and mysterious mutual funds, we have come a long way from the simpler, more transparent arrangements that were the norm when Willard Libby started investing.

And our lack of comprehension costs us dearly. According to data assembled for this book by the Bogle Financial Markets Research Center, the average mutual fund investor's return was about 40 percent lower than the stock market's overall return from 1983 to 2011.[17] Nevertheless, a 2012 research study showed that 80 percent of shareholders were confident in their mutual funds' ability to help them achieve their financial goals.[18]

With few alternatives in the market, investors have two choices—continue to sleep or wake up and change the system. Investors ultimately own the capital and have the power. It is absolutely within their right and capacity to step up and take back the power and responsibility.

The first step in reinvesting is to understand where we are and how we got here, to learn how the financial system got its hands on so much of our money—and with so few strings attached.

2

Sleepwalking into Retirement: The Shift from Pension to 401(k)

How did we end up here? How did financial firms and money managers get their hands on so much of our money in the first place? How did we get pushed to the sidelines of our own investing?

The saga began in 1875, when the American Express Company created the first corporate pension plan.[1] Though the particulars of pensions were different then, the general idea was roughly the same as today: businesses put a portion of workers' income in a collective savings account, invest the money, and use the proceeds to provide employees with guaranteed income after they retire. This is referred to as a *defined benefit plan*; the payment, usually a percentage of the worker's final salary, is defined in advance and pro-vided monthly until the employee dies.

Driven by a series of tax laws passed to make pensions more attractive to corporations, the defined benefit model proliferated in the 1920s. By 1929, there were nearly four hundred plans active in major North American corpora-tions, including US Steel, General Electric, Bethlehem Steel, and Eastman Kodak, Willard Libby's employer.[2] Pen-sions became a key tool for businesses in recruiting and retaining workers and, in some ways, helped build the archetype of the American dream. Find a job with a good pension, the story went, and you could work hard for forty years and then retire, move somewhere warm, and play bridge every day for the rest of your life.

Supported by another slew of favorable provisions added to the US tax code in the 1950s, federal and state government agencies and corporate employers founded defined benefit plans enthusiastically over the following decades. This was, in many ways, a real boon for the mid-dle class, as employers managed much of the cost, risk, and responsibility of workers' post-retirement finances.

As the cost of health care increased and life spans grew longer, however, companies began to struggle under the weight of these obligations. Over the course of a few decades, defined benefit plans transitioned from an effective tool for recruiting and retaining employees into a financial albatross for many companies.

Then, in 1963, the Studebaker Corporation, an American car manufacturer, blew the first real breeze into this house of cards. Roger Lowenstein summarized the story in a 2005 *New York Times* article, "The End of Pensions."

> *Companies might establish plans, but many were derelict when it came to funding them. When companies failed, the workers lost much of their promised benefit. The U.A.W. [United Auto Workers union] was acutely aware of the problem, because of the failing condition of several smaller car manufacturers. . . . The union didn't have the muscle to force full funding, and even if it did, it reckoned that if the weaker manufacturers were obliged to put more money into their pension funds, they would retaliate by cutting wages.*
>
> *Thus in 1959, Studebaker, a manufacturer fallen on hard times, agreed to increase benefits—its third such increase in six years. In return, the U.A.W. let Studebaker stretch out its pension funding schedule. This bargain preserved the union's wages, as*

well as management's hopes for a profit, though it required each to pretend that Studebaker could afford a pension plan that was clearly beyond its means. Four years later, the company collapsed.[3]

Studebaker was the first in a series of large US corporations to be overwhelmed by its pension burdens, default on employees and beneficiaries, and leave thousands of workers high and dry. Pension bankruptcies became a slow-motion crisis in the early 1960s, as an increasing number of corporations were revealed to have been incapable of managing their obligations for reasons that ranged from incompetence to recklessness to simple bad luck.

The US government launched an investigation into the raft of defaults, and in 1967, Senator Jacob Javits introduced legislation to develop stronger rules for governing the pension system. For years, business groups and labor unions fought him. But Javits was persistent, and in 1972, Congress was finally persuaded to hold a series of public hearings that would ultimately catalyze widespread support for reform.[4]

The Seeds of a New Model

In 1974, President Gerald Ford signed into law the Employee Retirement Income Security Act (ERISA). It dramatically changed the way Americans saved for retirement and, consequently, the way they invested, too.

I had a bird's-eye view of ERISA and its impact. My father, Robert A. G. Monks, was a founding trustee of the Federal Employees' Retirement System. He also served in the US Department of Labor as administrator of the office of the Pension and Welfare Benefits Program (now the Employee Benefits Security Administration), which oversaw the entire US pension system.

Importantly, ERISA codified the rules for how companies managed their retirement obligations and "enshrined the concept that pension promises were sacred."[5] For example, the law specified how much money had to be put aside in order to honor an obligation and mandated that companies demonstrate to beneficiaries that their pensions were being managed responsibly.

Another ERISA provision paved the way for a new type of savings plan: the individual retirement arrangement (IRA).

Designed to supplement retirement programs sponsored by employers (i.e., pensions), IRAs offered tax advantages to encourage workers to put aside money for retirement.

How It Works: The Individual Retirement Arrangement

The individual retirement arrangement is essentially a savings account with three special twists.[6] First, money you deposit into it is free from income taxation. Second, when you buy or sell stocks, bonds, or other securities with money in an IRA, you don't have to pay capital gains taxes on the earnings (as long as all the money stays in the account). Compare this with the standard 15 percent tax on the sale of securities and you see the appeal.

There's a trade-off for this tax advantage, however, and this is the third twist: you have to pay a 10 percent penalty plus capital gains taxes (which may be as high as 25 percent) on any money withdrawn before you reach age fifty-nine and a half. After that, you can withdraw your money without penalty, though you still have to pay income taxes on it.

The thinking is that if you're like most Americans, you're likely to be in a lower tax bracket after retirement than when you're in the prime of your career, and so the arrangement

*provides a considerable tax advantage. There are several dif-
ferent types of IRAs, including the Roth IRA and the SIMPLE
(Savings Incentive Match Plan for Employees) IRA, each of
which offers a different degree of flexibility and tax advantage.*

———

In establishing this new, tax-advantaged channel for Americans to save for retirement, ERISA opened a can of worms.
Intentionally or not, the IRA sowed the seeds of a lucrative
new market for financial firms: selling retirement products
and services directly to middle-class Americans. Within
just a few years, that market would metastasize through the
401(k) and set the stage for a new financial era.

Shift Happens:
Outsourcing Retirement Planning

With a wonky moniker befitting its origin in the IRS code,
the 401(k) provision was written into the books in 1978[7] and
essentially ignored until 1980, when a retirement benefits
consultant named Ted Benna discovered its potential to
reduce a client's tax burden. Originally applicable to highly

paid executives only, 401(k) eligibility was eventually expanded to all employees at all levels.

How It Works: The 401(k)

Much as a traditional IRA does, a 401(k) lets you defer a portion of your income into a tax-free savings account. Employees and employers can make pretax contributions that are not taxed while inside the account. It is also like an IRA in that capital gains taxes on earnings are excused as long as the proceeds remain in the account. Once the money is withdrawn, it's subject to income taxes. And as with an IRA, until you reach fifty-nine and a half, the money is locked up, and there are penalties to pay if you make early withdrawals.

Defined contribution plans like IRAs and 401(k)s gave employers a way to still support employees while shaving the cost and shedding the brunt of the responsibility of serving as their sole, or at least main, provider after retirement. Having staggered through two economic recessions during the first half of the 1970s, employers were eager to adopt this new model, and by 1980, nearly twenty million Americans were participating in defined contribution plans.[8]

Full of Bull: Outsourcing the Future

Financial corporations, smelling an opportunity, began to roll out new products and services to accommodate the nascent retirement-fund market. Playing on the insecurities of the growing population of Americans working without a defined benefit pension, financial firms and money managers marketed products, especially 401(k) plans, in ways that exploited both the fears and the hopes of a new generation of investors increasingly anxious about their capacity to provide for themselves and their families in retirement. Still, there was something appealing and quintessentially American in empowering individuals to be the masters of their own financial destinies.

The first few decades of the defined contribution era, from the early 1980s until the end of the twentieth century, seemed to validate this strategy of financial self-determination professionally stewarded by Wall Street. For about two decades, it appeared that outsourcing our financial affairs to money managers and financial corporations, through 401(k) plans and mutual funds, was going to deliver on its promise in spectacular fashion.

The economy was in overdrive, bolstered by a thriving

technology sector and appreciating housing market. Picking mutual funds, playing the stock market—it was all pretty easy. Year after year, account balances went up and up.

Until, of course, they went way, way down.

Looking back now, we can see that the great returns were largely transient, an illusion enabled by one of the great bull markets of the twentieth century. But the transformation in the infrastructure of retirement saving is permanent: by the end of the 1990s, IRAs and 401(k)s had surpassed defined benefit pensions in number, participants, and total assets (see the table below).[9]

Number of Plans, Participants, and Assets by Type of Plan, 1975–2010						
	Defined Benefit Plans			Defined Contribution Plans		
Year	Plans	Participants (thousands)	Assets (millions)	Plans	Participants (thousands)	Assets (millions)
1975	103,346	33,004	$185,950	207,748	11,507	$74,014
1980	148,096	37,979	401,455	340,805	19,924	162,096
1985	170,172	39,692	826,117	461,963	34,973	426,622
1990	113,062	38,832	961,904	599,245	38,091	712,236
1995	69,492	39,736	1,402,079	623,912	47,716	1,321,657
2000	48,773	41,613	1,986,177	686,878	61,716	2,216,495
2005	47,614	41,925	2,254,032	631,481	75,481	2,807,590
2010	46,543	41,423	2,448,361	654,469	88,301	3,833,388

Source: US Department of Labor, *Private Pension Plan Bullentin Historical Tables and Graphs*, various years

And in 2006, after a period of aggressive lobbying by the financial industry, the Pension Protection Act was signed into law, requiring employers to reserve even larger amounts of money to cover their defined benefit pensions while making no such demands on the financial corporations administrating and managing IRA and 401(k) plans. The new funding requirements for defined benefit pensions were akin to asking a homeowner to pay off a thirty-year mortgage in five years, and their impact hastened the demise of many plans. Total underfunding of all pension plans insured by the Pension Benefit Guaranty Corporation now exceeds $180 billion.[10]

The Pension Protection Act also made it easier for employers to automatically enroll employees in 401(k)s, and contributions continue to increase as a result[11]—by 13 percent from 2006 to 2013, according to the *Wall Street Journal*.[12] Tighter restrictions for defined benefit plans paired with looser rules for defined contribution plans made the predominance of the 401(k) today all but inevitable. In 1998, 90 percent of Fortune 100 companies offered defined benefit plans to new salaried employees.[13] By 2008, only 7 percent of private-sector employees with retirement benefits had a traditional defined benefit pension.[14]

After the Crash: A Financial Autopsy

In the wake of two more economic recessions, the data show that "professional" investment products and services may provide only illusory benefits to investors. As of 2010, three-quarters of Americans nearing retirement age had less than $30,000 in retirement savings.[15] Millions of baby boomers are financially underprepared for retirement. Ultimately, many of them will be unable to afford it. Though there are multiple factors contributing to this looming catastrophe, including a decreasing household savings rate and an increasingly challenging labor market (especially for older workers), the costs of modern investing, and particularly the fees, must be acknowledged.[16]

The IRA and 401(k) opened the door for money managers to sell complex financial products to consumers, most of whom did not comprehend what they were buying. Even today, most people lack even a rudimentary understanding of how these complicated plans work or how much they cost. According to a 2011 survey by the American Association of Retired Persons (AARP), 80 percent of respondents thought 401(k) plans were free or weren't sure whether they paid fees.[17]

The defined contribution model breathed life into an enormous market for financial firms. Though there's nothing inherently wrong with the IRA in and of itself, it has become the de facto investment for uninformed consumers who don't understand its costs or implications. And many firms that sell and manage IRAs and 401(k)s steer their customers into an investment designed specifically for people who don't know what they're doing—the mutual fund.

The 401(k) and IRA: Financial Honeypots

Many employers encourage employees to fund their 401(k) plan by matching a certain percentage of each employee's contributions. Though financial pundits and money managers often characterize this match as "free money," it obscures some of the drawbacks of participating in a 401(k).

One issue is that employees have only one choice: employers decide on a plan, and employees can decide to participate or not. Many plans, especially those offered to small businesses, feature high administration and management fees, which may be paid, sometimes unwittingly, by plan participants.[18] Only since July 2012 has the Labor

Department required 401(k) plan administrators to send participants a quarterly statement showing rates of returns, fees, and expenses.[19]

Another issue is that 401(k) advisers and administrators often double as brokers. In exchange for managing a company's 401(k) at a reduced cost, or for free, that administrator may be allowed to handpick the investments offered in the plan. In fact, the average corporate 401(k) includes ten or so investment options, which are most often mutual funds.[20] Employees may assume that the funds in their plan were selected by someone working in their best interest, but it's possible that a fund paid the administrator for its place on the menu in what's called a "revenue sharing" deal.[21]

IRA plans may also steer consumers into non-optimal investments. Fidelity offers a number of IRA plans that exempt customers from setup, maintenance, and transaction fees—as long as deposited funds are used to buy Fidelity mutual funds.[22] (Note that this specific example, like all the others in this book, is representative of a widespread, systemic practice rather than a unique transgression committed by one specific company.)

Fidelity's standard IRA plan requires a customer to make an initial deposit into a money market mutual fund or savings account. The default fund, Fidelity's Money Market

Fund, which had more than $2.4 billion under management in 2014, delivered a 0.01 percent return in that same year—but carried a 0.42 percent total expense ratio. Any way you look at them, those terms constitute a lousy investment. Sure, the savings account exempts the investor from the management fee.[23] But the 0.01 percent interest rate ensures that any minuscule return would immediately be lost to inflation.

Today the majority of middle-class retirement assets are held in defined contribution programs such as IRAs and 401(k)s. As of December 2014, US retirement assets totaled $24.2 trillion; 401(k) plans accounted for an estimated $4.5 trillion of this, or roughly 19 percent of the total (see Figure 6), and IRAs represented more than $7 trillion in assets (see Figure 7).[24]

Defined benefit pensions are rarely offered by new companies and startups today. Though the amount of assets held by these plans remains significant, especially in the government sector, the model creeps inevitably toward extinction. The risk and responsibility of saving for retirement has been shifted, perhaps permanently, from employers to employees.

When the economy was in full throttle and returns were high, the fees were less visible. For a time, it seemed

U.S. Total Retirement Market
Trillions of dollars, end-of-period, selected periods

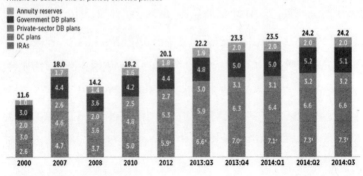

◦ Data are estimated.

Note: For definitions of plan categories, see Table 1 in "The U.S. Retirement Market, Third Quarter 2014." Components may not add to the total because of rounding.

Sources: Investment Company Institute, Federal Reserve Board, Department of Labor, National Association of Government Defined Contribution Administrators, American Council of Life Insurers, and Internal Revenue Service Statistics of Income Division

Figure 6. US Total Retirement Market, 2000–2014: Q2

401(k) Plan Assets
Trillions of dollars, end-of-period, selected periods

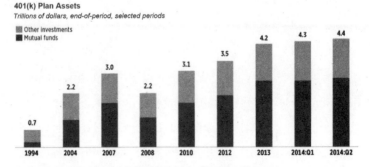

Sources: Investment Company Institute, Federal Reserve Board, and Department of Labor.

See Investment Company Institute, "The U.S. Retirement Market, Second Quarter 2014" (September 2014).

Figure 7. 401(k) Plan Assets, 1994–2014: Q2

that it would be possible to sleepwalk through the process and leave the actual investing to others. It has become increasingly clear, however, how costly this has been. Still, in the wake of two recessions in ten years, financial firms and money managers are trying to lull us back to sleep.

As the popularity of traditional defined benefit pensions faded out in the United States, investors were increasingly

left to fend for themselves without adequate protection. The shift from employer-managed pensions to individual choice and consumer sovereignty created a massive market of inexperienced but motivated investors.

Willard Libby, having taken his investing into his own hands, largely avoided the fees and other pitfalls of out-sourced ownership. Others may not have seen the danger. Or perhaps they thought that someone—their financial advisers, elected officials, or government regulators—would protect their interests and watch their backs.

This was not the case.

3

Who Watches While We Sleep?: From Watchdogs to Lapdogs

The decline of the defined benefit pension and the rise of the defined contribution model created an enormous market of new investors navigating the financial landscape for the first time. Lacking the confidence to build a portfolio on their own, most of these novices used 401(k) and IRA plans to invest in mutual funds, attracted to what seemed like a simple, trustworthy solution to a daunting challenge.

Unsurprisingly, the combination of inexperienced consumers and a marketplace rife with complexity, opacity, and asymmetry led to exploitation and abuse, bubbles and downturns, and a generation of investors whose financial aspirations have gone largely unattained. From this perspective, contemporary investors are in greater need than ever of the supervision and protection historically provided by government and other agents of accountability.

There are plenty of individuals and groups, public and private, working to promote transparency, protect consumer interests, and empower investors. Unfortunately, as time goes on, each of them is less equipped to match the ascendant economic resources, political influence, and institutional advantages of the financial industry. And as the financial universe continues to grow larger, more complex, and populated with ever more investors, the capacity of government and others to effectively police it is under increasing strain.

Big Brother Is Not Big Enough

The government remains an important and powerful check on the financial industry. While the US Department of Justice seeks to enforce the law and protect our rights as citizens and investors in the broadest terms, there is no shortage of federal agencies specifically dedicated to overseeing the financial sector.[1]

The Securities and Exchange Commission (SEC) works to "protect investors, maintain fair, orderly, and efficient markets, and facilitate capital formation."[2] The Commodity Futures Trading Commission toils to "protect market participants and the public from fraud, manipulation, abusive practices and systemic risk related to derivatives . . . and to foster transparent, open, competitive and financially sound markets."[3] The Consumer Financial Protection Bureau, established in 2011, is the newest government watchdog charged with enforcing financial laws.[4]

Despite all this governmental manpower, the legislative and regulatory processes have been fundamentally and thoroughly compromised by many of the same issues undermining the financial sector: complexity, conflicts of interest, and the corrupting influence of money.

The Dodd-Frank Wall Street Reform and Consumer Protection Act, signed into law by President Barack Obama on July 21, 2010, exemplifies many of the limits of legislation and regulation. Designed to "promote the financial stability of the United States by improving accountability and transparency in the financial system," the law seeks "to protect consumers from abusive financial services practices."[5]

As of July 2013, the 848-page Dodd-Frank bill had yielded more than 15 million words of new law. Ten different regulators had contributed to the law's 13,789 pages of rules, of which 2,100 pages were dedicated to consumer protection and 5,000 pages addressed derivatives alone.[6] Regulation Z under the Truth in Lending Act, now administered by the Consumer Financial Protection Bureau, is 313 pages long. Despite, or perhaps because of this, the law's implementation was still less than 60 percent complete as of December 2014.[7]

In an interview for this book, we asked Barney Frank whether a full implementation of the bill as written would solve the problems it was designed to address. He said, "It would make it very, very, very unlikely that we would have a repeat of past practices. Very unlikely that you would see further irresponsibility with capital requirements—and absolute prohibition against any use of taxpayer dollars to keep [companies] alive, the bailout thing.

"The Tea Party got it partly right; we did have 'death panels' in our legislation in 2010. But it was for big banks—not old ladies. The bailouts that we had in 2008—they have all been made illegal. What could happen, however, is that you will get a right-wing administration that will appoint people who won't use the rules."

Of course, this is exactly what happened. Factions of the government itself have mitigated the efficacy of Dodd-

Frank by starving federal and state agencies of the resources they need to provide effective oversight.

This is a major drawback inherent in the legislative approach. In trying to set out specific rules for every situation and scenario, the rule-making process may only reflect the complexity of the financial sector instead of reining it

in. Regulation can perpetuate the cycle of well-resourced money managers and financial corporations searching for and finding loopholes to exploit. In July 2014, four years after the bill's passage, "the top six bank holding companies [were] 37 percent larger than they were before the 2008 crisis," according to the *New York Times*.[8]

Too Influential, High-Tech, and International to Fail

The sheer volume and complexity of US financial legislation makes it hard to digest for investors and corporations alike. The way legislation is shaped, and the role of money in the political process, are other problems. Corporate contributions accounted for one-third of the $6 billion spent on the 2012 presidential election.[9] Since 1998, the financial sector has spent more than $4.2 billion on lobbying.[10] And in the wake of Citizens United's victory over the Federal Election Commission in its 2010 Supreme Court case, the influence of special interests in policy making continues to accelerate in tandem with corporate spending on political advocacy.[11]

In addition, the revolving door between Congress and corporations, especially large financial services firms, further undermines the prospect of effective oversight. In 2014, the Center for Responsive Politics counted more than 700 lobbyists for the securities and investment industry, including more than 450 "revolvers"—alumni of congressional offices and former federal employees working as lobbyists for the financial sector.[12]

Technology is another area in which the financial sector has massive advantages over the government. The rollout of the Affordable Care Act's online platform, HealthCare.gov, showcased the limits of the government's technological aptitude.

Meanwhile, with billions of dollars in annual profits to invest in infrastructure, research, and salaries, financial firms attract the brightest minds. From hedge funds to high-frequency-trading firms to institutional investors, financial corporations remain at the vanguard of information technology, running circles around our elected officials and regulators.

In addition, many important regulations were engineered decades ago for a manufacturing-based economy— not one based on increasingly fast-paced exchanges of information and arcane financial engineering. Given this, the government is doomed to perpetually play catch-up, designing this year's regulations to address last year's problems.

As the economy becomes increasingly globalized, the challenge of striking the right balance between financial regulation and free enterprise grows more complex. The economic crisis of 2008 highlighted the many real drawbacks of the increasing speed and interconnectedness of business and, especially, finance. A Department of the Treasury report published in 2009 summarizes some of the problems: "Financial stress can spread easily and quickly across national boundaries. Yet, regulation is still set largely in a national context. Without consistent supervision and regulation, financial institutions will tend to move their activities to jurisdictions with looser standards, creating a race to the bottom and intensifying systemic risk for the entire global financial system."[13]

The framing of the problem is dead-on, but the earnest notion of "consistent supervision and regulation" is a chimera. Government, lacking the resources to monitor what is an essentially virtual and invisible business, is, on a purely practical level, incapable of providing either—even if members of Congress were interested in doing so.

Other Agents of Accountability in Peril

In addition to the protection ostensibly offered by securities laws, regulatory agencies, and courts, investors have long relied on the work of accounting firms, credit-rating agencies, and self-regulating organizations such as the Financial Industry Regulatory Authority. Though all these parties have the potential to provide supervision, enforce the rules, and promote accuracy and accountability, they have all been neutralized by fundamental and entrenched conflicts of interest.

Accounting is the language of business, and bookkeeping and auditing are among the most important ways in which corporations communicate financial information. Internally, accounting is crucial to business operations and executive decision making; externally, it's a vital source of information for investors and governments. Given this, it's important for accounting information to accurately and comprehensively reflect the reality of business activity and performance.

Reporting requirements are designed to give investors and other stakeholders confidence in the truthfulness of a corporation's stated financial position and performance;

having an objective third party such as an accounting firm corroborate those statements through auditing provides reassurance to investors who base decisions on them.

In 2001 and 2002, a series of scandals at Enron, World-Com, and a prominent accounting firm revealed fundamental flaws in financial disclosure rules that undermined the trustworthiness of accounting standards and practices. The scandals cost employees, investors, and taxpayers billions of dollars, damaged public confidence in the securities markets, and highlighted the challenge of regulating quickly changing markets.

Despite the implementation of a number of reforms since then, the accounting and auditing process remains fundamentally flawed. When corporations pay accounting firms for services, as most do today, accountants cannot reliably perform their critical duties as impartial, independent agents. In this context, accounting firms unwilling to deliver findings that square with corporate expectations lose clients.

The conflicts of interest that permit "creative" accounting lead to inaccurate analyses of risk. As corporate law professor John Coffee writes, "Watchdogs hired by those they are to watch typically turn into pets, not guardians."[14] The economic relationship between the auditor and the audited undermines the basic credibility of the process. In this situation, accounting makes a charade of accountability and gives investors false confidence.

Similarly, credit-rating agencies supposedly assess the creditworthiness of issuers of corporate debt, municipal bonds, and financial instruments like mortgage-backed securities. Investors routinely use these ratings to determine the risk of an investment; those with lower ratings usually pay higher interest rates.

In the early twentieth century, the first agencies—Moody's, Standard & Poor's, and Fitch—sold ratings directly to investors. After the 1929 stock market crash, the federal government increasingly relied on the "big three" to provide bond quality assessments for banks and insurance companies. As photocopying technology became more widely available in the 1970s, making it easy for customers to reproduce rating manuals, the agencies' changed their business model. Instead of selling information to bond buyers, they began to sell ratings directly to corporations issuing securities.

As with accounting, a flawed compensation structure undermines the credit-rating business. Corporations purchase credit ratings for the bonds and other securities they sell; as the agencies' customers, corporations can essentially shop around for the ratings they want. This arrangement is exceedingly vulnerable to corruption, and ratings are routinely awarded to keep clients happy rather than issued as honest, unbiased assessments of risk.

In our interview with Barney Frank, he blamed the rating agencies for contributing to the financial scandal of 2008. "If you want to use them, fine," he said, "but they had become a substitute for people thinking for themselves."

Dependent on their corporate masters, accounting firms, auditors, and credit-rating agencies have become a dangerous source of misinformation, and investors and their money managers should recognize this when basing investment decisions on their analyses.

Self-regulatory organizations (SROs) can augment government regulatory efforts through the development and enforcement of codes of conduct, best practices, and compliance standards at the industry level. SROs have played a prominent role in the securities industry; stock exchanges were among the first self-regulating bodies, offering traders access to a marketplace that provided infrastructure and rules of conduct, as well as some measure of accountability.

The Financial Industry Regulatory Authority (FINRA) is among the largest self-regulatory organizations in the United States, with more than 3,200 employees overseeing 4,100 securities firms and more than 639,000 brokers.[15] Though it ostensibly serves as a referee for the financial industry, including accounting firms and credit-rating agencies, FINRA is funded by the very industry it presumes to oversee.

In 2010 and 2011, FINRA spent $2 million lobbying Congress in an effort to expand its purview to investment advisers—a group already challenged by conflicts of interest that could benefit from more oversight, not less.[16] Still, the government may lack a better alternative. Though Dodd-Frank calls for expanded oversight, the SEC received only a 2 percent budget increase in 2014—far short of the 26 percent increase it requested.[17]

Barney Frank characterized the situation this way: "The Republican argument was that the SEC doesn't have enough money to do its job, so let's expand FINRA. Well, why doesn't the SEC have enough money to do its job? It's not that there's a lack of money in the world. Two days in Afghanistan would fund it.

"You just don't want to give it to them."

An Impossible Job

Americans are in a tough spot. Many of us distrust the financial industry. Even if we believe that government must help keep it accountable, we increasingly doubt its capacity to do so effectively.

Our regulatory policy reflects confusion. Scandals and periods of excess lead to renewed calls for governmental intervention; periods of calm inevitably lead to a loosening of the rules. The ideological struggle between business and government, regulation and deregulation, has created an inconsistent, reactive policy that invites unintended consequences and economic friction without effectively protecting us from corruption and abuse.

Investors need protection from money managers and financial corporations. Recent history has clearly demonstrated that our system requires a strong network of public and private agents of accountability to protect society, the environment, and the economy. Unfortunately, many of the safeguards we have relied on in the past are no longer adequate.

The truth is that no one is watching while investors sleep.

4

Mutual Funds: The Big Sleep

In an environment largely free of government supervision and regulatory interference, financial firms pounced. Emboldened by widespread investor confusion and inexperience, money managers steered clients in massive numbers into IRAs and 401(k) plans. Once they had them enrolled, it was relatively easy for plan administrators to present their captive investors with a limited menu of choices. Most of these were mutual funds, one of the financial industry's most profitable products.

Today, more than 60 percent of total 401(k) assets are held in mutual funds. IRA owners are more likely to hold mutual funds in their portfolios than any other type of investment.[1] Although the reach of the mutual fund owes much to its deep roots in the 401(k) and IRA businesses, it transcends them.

Roughly 92 million Americans—more than one in three adults in the United States—invest in mutual funds. As of September 2014, the industry collectively controlled more than $15 trillion. With US household assets totaling roughly $76 trillion, roughly 20 cents out of every dollar Americans have to their collective name is invested in mutual funds.[2]

On the surface, the mutual fund model makes intuitive sense. Its patina of practicality, which is played off the average investor's insecurities, has made it the era's default investment.

What exactly *are* mutual funds, anyway? Industry powerhouse Fidelity defines them as "investment strategies that allow you to pool your money together with other investors to purchase a collection of stocks, bonds, or other securities that might be difficult to recreate on your own."[3] At the most elementary level, a mutual fund is just a money manager's handpicked portfolio of stocks or bonds, purchased with a group of investors' money.

Because most funds have many hundreds or thousands of shareholders, economies of scale defray the costs and effort of investing across a broad base, or so the story goes.

With size comes the appearance of efficiency, strength, and safety.

For the uninformed investor, one of the most attractive features of the mutual fund is that it comes with built-in professional financial advice. In a strategy known as *active management,* a mutual fund manager selects between one hundred and two hundred securities. Actively managed mutual funds marry investment with guidance; every share itself is a marketable security, professionally managed.

In contrast to conventional mutual funds, index funds and exchange-traded funds (ETFs) are passively managed—designed to match the returns of a specific group of securities, such as the S&P 500 or the Russell 5000 index, without a fund manager's intervention. Index funds buy and sell securities relatively infrequently, making them more tax efficient on average than mutual funds. ETFs also track an index (or group of assets) but are priced in real time, unlike a mutual fund, which is priced once a day.

There are other inviting features. Mutual funds are highly liquid, which means they're very easy to buy and sell, especially compared to some other assets such as real estate and jewelry. They also provide a shortcut to diversification; one share of a fund gives an investor exposure to hundreds of securities across a variety of industries, geographies, and other categories.

The industry's conventional argument is that buying mutual funds is less risky for investors than buying stocks, which tethers one's destiny to the performance of a handful of businesses. Of course, the diversity of mutual funds also limits the potential upside.

Mutual funds are also accessible. Investing in a hedge

The case for mutual funds

For the average small investor, mutual funds can be a smart and cost-effective way to invest. You don't have to have a lot of money—most funds will let you buy shares with as little as $2,000 up front and invest as little as $50 per month. Buying shares in a mutual fund is also an easy way to help diversify your investments, which is really another way of saying that you won't have all your eggs in one basket. For instance, most mutual funds hold well over 100 securities. For someone with just a few thousand dollars to invest, building and managing a portfolio containing that many securities could potentially be highly impractical, if not impossible.

Professional management

As a mutual fund investor, you get the benefit of having a professional manager reviewing the portfolio on an ongoing basis. Professional portfolio managers and analysts have the expertise and technology resources needed to research companies and analyze market information before making investment decisions. Fund managers identify which securities to buy and sell through individual security evaluation, sector allocation, and analysis of technical factors. For those who have neither the time nor the expertise to oversee their investments, this can potentially be invaluable.

Liquidity and convenience

All mutual funds allow you to buy or sell your fund shares once a day at the close of the market at the fund's NAV. You can also automatically reinvest income from dividends and capital gain distributions or make additional investments at any time. For most stock funds, the required minimum initial investment may be substantially less than what you would have to invest to build a diversified portfolio of individual stocks.

Fidelity.com: What Are Mutual Funds?

fund or private equity fund typically requires tens or hundreds of thousands of dollars, making them too expensive for most middle-class people. In most cases, however, an investor can buy into a mutual fund with as little as $2,000.[4]

Though $2,000 may constitute entry-level in the world of financial "solutions," purchasing stocks and bonds directly can be done for far less. Willard Libby's approach— buying the securities outright instead of a money manager's repackaged, securitized mash-up of investments—starts at a lower price, takes no more time or effort than selecting a mutual fund, and costs far less in fees.

The Financial Literacy Paradox

In addition to making it easier for novices to invest, mutual funds protect investors from some of the complex demands of modern finance. A mutual fund shields you from needing to *really* understand stocks and bonds, asset allocation and diversification, capitalizations and interest rates— subjects that can overwhelm someone without experience in business or finance.

Or does it?

Here is the fundamental paradox. Part of the value proposition in investing in a mutual fund is that you need not know much about finance. But you still have to know enough to choose a mutual fund from a market of more than seven thousand.[5] And to responsibly select a mutual fund, you have to grapple with complicated topics such as net asset values, expense ratios, back-end load fees, commissions, dollar cost averaging, and turnover rates.

If you consult a financial adviser for help with choosing a mutual fund, you still need to understand how to choose a financial adviser. You have to consider how advisers calculate and report their fees, their incentives and compensation models, the implications of their fiduciary obligations, and so on.

And you must do all this so you need not worry about not having financial expertise in the first place! In this sense, mutual funds offer investors little more than psychological cover.

Investors often take comfort in their money managers' confidence. The alternative is to acknowledge the frightening truth that no one can predict the future—especially of something as complex and volatile as the stock market or economy. But when we invest in mutual funds, we

One-on-One Guidance

Personal guidance is available to all Schwab clients, at no additional cost. Get the one-on-one help you need to make smart decisions with your money.

Personal Portfolio Review

As a Schwab client, you can schedule your Personal Portfolio Review to:

- Discuss your goals, both short-term and long-term.
- Evaluate your current investments relative to your goals.
- Get specific recommendations and next steps.

Call ▮▮▮▮▮▮▮ to schedule your consultation. There is no cost to you, and no obligation to follow any of the investment recommendations.

In order that we may provide a detailed set of portfolio recommendations, Personal Portfolio Review is available to clients with $25,000 or more in assets at Schwab.

For assets under $25,000, we offer All-in-One Portfolio Solutions and 24/7 Help with your investments.

How we help you

Fresh Perspective

We'll review and discuss your financial situation and help you set goals.

Portfolio Review

Offer our thoughts on your portfolio's allocation and the right investment mix for you.

Specific Recommendations

Suggest specific next steps, discuss potential solutions, and provide ways to help you stay on track.

Schwab.com: One-on-one Guidance

surrender our rights and responsibilities as investors. Our purchase of mutual funds irrevocably disconnects us from our investing.

This is not to suggest that mutual fund shareholders are lazy, lack interest, or don't care. Rather, it's evidence of the mutual fund as a very effective enabler, expertly marketed as the solution to a problem—lack of financial expertise—while perpetuating and exacerbating that very problem.

In an interview for this book, Vanguard founder Jack Bogle described the dynamic. "We've entered into this idea that investing is so complicated that you need expert help, and that's kind of embedded in almost the Puritan ethic," he said. "You've got a manager who works hard, it's certainly better than not having any manager at all.

"Except it isn't!"

Willard Libby didn't pay someone else. He did his own homework. He read his own financial statements. He invested in companies in which he believed. And if he didn't understand the business, he didn't invest.

The Murky Mechanics of Financial Advice

To drive sales, mutual fund companies have built a multi-faceted distribution network. You can buy shares on a fund's website, from representatives in retail branch locations, from your employers' IRA or 401(k) manager, or from a money manager.

Not all sources of financial advice are created equal, however.

According to the Aite Group, a financial research and advisory company, there are about 450,000 people in the United States offering financial guidance to consumers. Though they go by a variety of names—money manager, financial adviser, financial planner, and so on—roughly 90 percent of them are salespeople; *brokers* in the parlance of the industry. Only about 10 percent of financial advisers are *registered investment advisers* (RIAs).[6]

Though they may look alike, RIAs and brokers provide financial advice in different ways, for different reasons, and according to different rules. RIAs adhere to the *fiduciary standard*, which ethically and legally obligates them to put their clients' interests above their own. In contrast, brokers are required only to recommend investments that are "suitable" for their customers. This means that brokers can recommend higher-priced products or services, which typically earn them higher commissions, even if they are aware of comparable, lower-cost alternatives.

The SEC, a US government agency, regulates RIAs. Brokers are supervised by FINRA, a self-regulating organization funded and managed by financial corporations.

Brokers often populate the branches of firms such as Charles Schwab, Bank of America, and Wells Fargo. Though mutual funds have a fiduciary duty to uphold shareholders' interests first, they also compensate brokers, who have no such duty, to sell their shares to investors. As a result, when you walk into Bank of America, the customer service representative is probably being paid more to sell certain products and services than others.

Willard Libby told us that he avoided brokers' recommendations. "I'm afraid I didn't have a very high regard for brokers," he explained. "They were salesmen."

Investing with Eyes Wide Shut

Brokers and other mutual fund salespeople perpetuate the perception that real investing is too complex for the layperson. In fact, the mutual funds they sell are incredibly difficult to comprehend. And the language they use to communicate in prospectuses underscores their extreme complexity.

From the perspective of the average investor, the literature of finance seems designed not to enhance understanding but to repel it. You might imagine that a mutual fund prospectus, with its financial, legal, and technical jargon, is written that way to satisfy legal requirements or the demands of regulators.

In 2008, however, the SEC adopted a rule explicitly requiring mutual fund summary prospectuses to be written

A fund may also buy and sell options on swaps (swaptions), which are generally options on interest rate swaps. An option on a swap gives a party the right (but not the obligation) to enter into a new swap agreement or to extend, shorten, cancel or modify an existing contract at a specific date in the future in exchange for a premium. Depending on the terms of the particular option agreement, a fund will generally incur a greater degree of risk when it writes (sells) an option on a swap than it will incur when it purchases an option on a swap. When a fund purchases an option on a swap, it risks losing only the amount of the premium it has paid should it decide to let the option expire unexercised. However, when a fund writes an option on a swap, upon exercise of the option the fund will become obligated according to the terms of the underlying agreement. A fund that writes an option on a swap receives the premium and bears the risk of unfavorable changes in the preset rate on the underlying interest rate swap. Whether a fund's use of options on swaps will be successful in furthering its investment objective will depend on the adviser's ability to predict correctly whether certain types of investments are likely to produce greater returns than other investments. Options on swaps may involve risks similar to those discussed below in "Swap Agreements."

Fidelity Freedom 2040 Fund Statement of Additional Information (excerpt)

in "plain English."[7] In 2011, the commission enacted rules requiring financial advisers (including mutual fund companies) to include "plain English" descriptions of their investment philosophies, fees, and possible conflicts of interest.[8]

Do you consider the language used in the Fidelity Freedom 2040 Fund's *Statement of Additional Information,* above, to be plain English?

The fact that the plain English rules were first adopted in 2008 is confounding. That they were applied only to the prospectus summary, and excluded the full prospectus and other important documents, defies common sense.

Nevertheless, even with the plain English mandate, most mutual fund documentation still fails utterly to convey information clearly, concisely, or in any way that an average investor could reasonably be expected to comprehend. Rather, it bewilders readers before burying them under an avalanche of circular, self-referential, and arcane language.

———

In 1963, Ned Johnson, the founder of Fidelity, established the Magellan Fund. It was once the largest mutual fund on earth. As of December 2014, the Magellan Fund had $16.7 billion under management[9] out of Fidelity's mutual fund total of $1.74 trillion.[10]

In an interview for this book, Vanguard founder Jack Bogle imagined the following scene:

> *Ned C. Johnson, up in Boston, runs a firm called Fidelity. One day he says to his guys, "Vanguard is eating our lunch! They used to be $200 billion behind us and now they're $600 billion ahead of us—$600 billion!" He says, "We're going to go eat their lunch. So I want you guys to talk to all our people, and I want you to come back and give me a solution."*

So the guys come back and they say, "First of all, your profit is gone." Fidelity made two and a half billion last year, and the Johnson family is probably 30 percent of that. So you're not going to do that kind of billion dollars a year, sorry to tell you about that. "Second, we're going to have to get big into the index business and we're going to have to undercut Vanguard. Third, we might as well fire half of the research staff. Then, no more marketing, no more hot television ads, no more green pathways—all of that will be cut out. And THAT can get us from a 1 percent expense ratio to 0.5 percent."

And Ned looks at them, and says, "Are you guys nuts? We do all that, we'll ruin the firm! So what we're going to do is nothing and enjoy the fruits of this great cash cow, for as long as it lasts, until it goes away."

Collectively, the 2013 editions of the Magellan prospectus and statement of additional information contain more than sixty-three thousand words. The annual report and semi-annual report together exceed twenty-seven thousand words. It would take an average person roughly five hours to read those documents once if they were written in standard, intelligible English.[11]

The literature of the mutual fund is schizophrenic, full of odd juxtapositions, mixed messages, and exorbitant tedium. The Magellan prospectus brims with legal and technical definitions, peculiar wording, and vague statements that resist comprehension. It is designed to persuade a reader to put it aside.

For example, here's the first chunk of text to greet you in this Magellan Fund prospectus supplement:

**Supplement to the
Fidelity® Magellan® Fund
May 30, 2013
Prospectus**

Effective January 18, 2014, if you hold your shares in a Fidelity mutual fund account and your dividend and/or redemption check(s) remains uncashed for six months, the check(s) may be reinvested in additional shares at the NAV next calculated on the day of the investment.

Previously, the group fee rate component of certain Fidelity funds' management fees was based on the monthly average net assets of all of the registered investment companies with which FMR has management contracts. Going forward, FMR has agreed that assets of Fidelity's sector funds that previously counted toward group assets will continue to be counted even after Fidelity SelectCo, LLC, an affiliate of FMR, has assumed management responsibilities for certain sector funds.

The following information replaces similar information in the Fund Management Section:

The group fee rate is based on the average net assets of all the mutual funds advised by FMR. For this purpose, the average net assets of any mutual funds previously advised by FMR that currently are advised by Fidelity SelectCo, LLC are included.

Any English major will tell you that every piece of writing should start with a strong, clear thesis statement. First impressions are important. What does Fidelity's introductory note say to you?

Next comes this message:

Like securities of all mutual funds, these securities have not been approved or disapproved by the Securities and Exchange Commission, and the Securities and Exchange Commission has not determined if this prospectus is accurate or complete. Any representation to the contrary is a criminal offense.

245 Summer Street, Boston, MA 02210

In other words, the government agency charged with regulating the securities industry has no opinion regarding the validity of this document, which may be inaccurate and incomplete. Good to know!

Next comes the statement of fund investment objectives:

Investment Objective

The fund seeks capital appreciation.

The fund will try to make money. That's great!

And here's how the prospectus describes the basics of how the fund will be managed:

Fund Services

Fund Management

The fund is a mutual fund, an investment that pools shareholders' money and invests it toward a specific goal.

The Adviser is the fund's manager. The address of the Adviser and its affiliates, unless otherwise indicated below, is 245 Summer Street, Boston, Massachusetts 02210.

As of December 31, 2013, the Adviser had approximately $881.7 million in discretionary assets under management, and approximately $1.94 trillion when combined with all of its affiliates' assets under management.

As the manager, the Adviser has overall responsibility for directing the fund's investments and handling its business affairs.

FMRC serves as a sub-adviser for the fund. FMRC has day-to-day responsibility for choosing investments for the fund.

FMRC is an affiliate of the Adviser. As of December 31, 2013, FMRC had approximately $866.5 billion in discretionary assets under management.

Other investment advisers assist the Adviser with foreign investments:

• Fidelity Management & Research (U.K.) Inc. (FMR U.K.), at 1 St. Martin's Le Grand, London, EC1A 4AS, United Kingdom, serves as a sub-adviser for the fund. As of December 31, 2013, FMR U.K. had approximately $23.3 billion in discretionary assets under management. FMR U.K. may provide investment research and advice on issuers based outside the United States and may also provide investment advisory services for the fund. FMR U.K. is an affiliate of the Adviser.

• Fidelity Management & Research (Hong Kong) Limited (FMR H.K.), at Floor 19, 41 Connaught Road Central, Hong Kong, serves as a sub-adviser for the fund. As of December 31, 2013, FMR H.K. had approximately $8.8 billion in discretionary assets under management. FMR H.K. may provide investment research and advice on issuers based outside the United States and may also provide investment advisory services for the fund. FMR H.K. is an affiliate of the Adviser.

• Fidelity Management & Research (Japan) Inc. (FMR Japan), at Kamiyacho Prime Place, 1-17, Toranomon-4-Chome, Minato-ku, Tokyo, Japan, serves as a sub-adviser for the fund. FMR Japan was organized in 2008 to provide investment research and advice on issuers based outside the United States. FMR Japan may provide investment research and advice on issuers based outside the United States and may also provide investment advisory services for the fund. FMR Japan is an affiliate of the Adviser.

▬▬▬▬▬▬▬ is portfolio manager of the fund, which he has managed since ▬▬▬▬▬▬. Since joining Fidelity Investments in ▬▬, Mr. ▬▬▬▬▬ has worked as a research analyst and portfolio manager.

The statement of additional information (SAI) provides additional information about the compensation of, and other accounts managed by, and any fund shares held by the portfolio manager.

Did you learn what you would want to know about this mutual fund? Did Fidelity explain what types of companies the Magellan Fund invests in? The rationale behind the securities it buys and sells?

How about the managers of this fund? Do they manage other funds? If so, how many other funds? How much is each manager paid in base compensation? How much are they paid in bonuses? How are bonuses calculated? Do the managers invest their own money in the Magellan Fund? It's striking that Fidelity left so many of the really interesting questions unanswered in such an extensive prospectus. (In fact, answers to a number of these questions are buried in the fund's 56-page *Statement of Additional Information*.)

And there are so very many crucial details tucked among the thirty-nine thousand words of dense legalese in the fund's *Statement of Additional Information*, including fourteen instances of the phrase "conflict of interest." Most investors would want to know about those conflicts of interest. But would they be steadfast enough to find them?

Behind mutual funds' superficial sheen of simplicity is deep complexity. And the funds' own prospectuses prove it.

We believe most investors really *do* want to understand how their money is being invested. But the vast majority of financial communication is designed not to shed light but to cast shade. This is intentional; unseemly details can be hidden in complexity. The legal and technical language characteristic of any mutual fund prospectus ensures that the average investor skips right over it.

Of course, corporate financial statements and annual reports are often riddled with the same type of financial jargon that plagues mutual fund prospectuses. But investors have a choice: read about the businesses in which they invest, as Willard did, or read a money manager's rationalization of his stock-picking strategy and all the fees he is going to charge you.

In an interview for this book, James Kaplan, a corporate governance and forensic accounting expert, told this story:

> I had looked at Enron. I had been a portfolio manager investor for many years and had looked at their prospectus. I was actually one of those people who still did that. At that time, there were more people who did that—now no one gives a shit. [The Enron prospectus] was too thick, it weighed a few pounds. I looked at it and said, there's no way in God's name I can look at this and understand it. It's way, way too thick. I flipped through it and

there were so many footnotes. I just threw it in the garbage and said, I'm not going to invest in it. I knew it was the seventh-largest company with only seven thousand employees and very magical. Very magical! I said this makes no sense.

Too Big to Know

"Buy what you know." This is an enduring axiom of conventional investment wisdom, originally attributed to legendary Fidelity mutual fund manager Peter Lynch.[12] Ironically, the very structure of mutual funds makes it difficult for investors to keep track of what they own.

The average equity mutual fund holds many dozens of stocks at any given time. The typical index fund, by definition, holds hundreds. It's virtually impossible for anyone to keep tabs on so many companies, let alone comprehend the cumulative scope of business activities involved. Even acknowledging that impossibility assumes that mutual fund companies actually tell their shareholders the names of the securities in which they've invested. Often they do not.

Some mutual funds publish a list of their holdings by

major market sector; others list some or all of the individual company names and the percentage that each represents in the fund portfolio. For example, Fidelity's Growth Discovery Fund lists only its top 10 investments (out of 135 in total as of December 2014), which account for about one-third of its total holdings, once per quarter.

As a result, shareholders don't know where two-thirds of their money has been invested. Furthermore, the Growth Discovery Fund has a 70 percent turnover rate (as of June 2014), which means that it sells seven out of ten holdings

Top 10 Holdings

AS OF 12/31/2014

35.03% TOP 10 HOLDINGS

FACEBOOK INC A

APPLE INC

GILEAD SCIENCES INC

KEURIG GREEN MOUNTAIN INC

ACTAVIS PLC

GOOGLE INC CL C

DANAHER CORP

BLACKSTONE GROUP LP

UNITED TECHNOLOGIES CORP

PROCTER & GAMBLE CO

% of Total Portfolio   **35.03%**

Total # of holdings: 135 as of 12/31/2014
Total # of issuers: 129 as of 12/31/2014

Fidelity Growth Discovery Fund, Top 10 Holdings, December 2014

every year. By the time Fidelity publishes updates to the pro-spectus, the compositional details therein may be outdated.

Note that a turnover rate of 70 percent is only slightly higher than the industry average of 61 percent for equity mutual funds from 1980 to 2013 (see Figure 8).[13] This higher turnover rate, of course, translates to more transaction costs, which result in higher costs overall for investors.

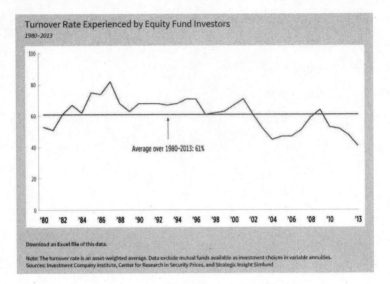

Figure 8. Equity Fund Turnover Rate, 1980–2013

Some mutual funds don't furnish *any* details about their holdings to shareholders. This "secret sauce" approach to investing, in which the portfolio is partially or fully obscured behind the cover of a "proprietary" trading strategy, makes it impossible for shareholders to know exactly where their money is invested. It also severely limits investors' capacity to hold fund managers accountable. If you don't know what you've invested in, you can't really judge performance.

Even if a mutual fund reports all of its holdings to investors, the sheer scale of the typical portfolio makes it difficult for an average investor to evaluate, let alone keep track of, what they own. Fidelity's own primer on mutual funds points out that for someone who has "just a few thousand dollars to invest, building and managing a portfolio containing [more than 100] securities could potentially be highly impractical, if not impossible."[14]

The situation being what it is, investors have no choice but to rely on funds to make decisions in their best interest. And mutual funds often talk about the safeguards they put in place to support the interests of shareholders. But given the lack of transparency in their communication, how can we be sure they are protecting our interests?

At the top of the corporate pile is a fund's parent company, also known as a fund sponsor, family, or complex. The Fidelity Investments complex sells shares of its Magellan Fund, for example. (Technically, a mutual fund has no employees and no internal operations. In fact, just about everything a mutual fund does, including its ostensible raison d'être—investment strategy and selection—is outsourced to either a third party or a separate division of its parent company.)

The corporate leadership of the fund complex then nominates and elects a board of directors to supervise fund management and operation on behalf of shareholders.

Typically, a fund family's corporate leadership has exclusive control of a fund's inaugural board composition, as it is the sole shareholder. Thereafter, management can effectively call the shots with regard to subsequent board nomination and membership. But not every fund has its *own* board of directors. Instead, fund directors typically serve as a trustee for *each and every fund in a complex simultaneously.* At Fidelity, the same board of directors oversees each of the complex's more than 200 stock funds; one other board supervises each of its 188 bond and money market funds.[15]

One of the board's most important tasks is hiring a company, the *fund adviser,* to manage its investment portfolio; note that this is often another division of the same parent company. The adviser then appoints a *portfolio manager* to make investment decisions for each fund. Each of Fidelity's more than 500 funds—or rather, their shareholders—pays Fidelity Management and Research LLC, a separate division of the company, to provide investment advice.

To safeguard shareholder interests, the board is in charge of evaluating and compensating the fund adviser; valuing the fund's securities; and signing off on statements of disclosure such as the prospectus and other regulatory documents. The board is also supposed to make sure the fund delivers satisfactory returns, charges reasonable fees, and represents shareholder interests in dealing with the corporations in which it invests.

Can a director overseeing two hundred funds reasonably be expected to read and digest every prospectus and regulatory filing and evaluate every strategy and compliance document? Can a fund manager and board of directors reasonably expect to track, manage, and oversee so many holdings?

In an interview with the *Wall Street Journal*, a Fidelity spokesperson defended the arrangement, suggesting that the "system works well for shareholders," because of the similar needs for research and consistency in pricing among funds.[16] In the same article, a spokesperson for the Vanguard Group, which has one board overseeing its entire line of funds, argued that having one board makes it simpler to deal with regulators.

In our interview with Vanguard founder Jack Bogle, he questioned the capacity of board members to provide fiduciary oversight for so many funds at once:

Take Fidelity or, for that matter, take Vanguard. We each run a couple hundred funds. Can our directors be fiduciaries and totally understand the workings of 160 or 260 different mutual funds? How can they be [an effective] fiduciary when they've got 160 oversights? I leave that as a question—but the answer is pretty obvious.[17]

The answer *is* obvious: they can't! There's no way for investors, fund managers, or boards of directors (not to mention regulators and government agencies) to comprehensively oversee a mutual fund invested in many hundreds of companies across multiple sectors and geographies. A fund director—overseeing hundreds of funds, each in turn investing in hundreds of companies—has an impossible supervisory responsibility.

From this perspective, index funds and ETFs are even worse for investors than actively managed funds. Though passively managed funds may charge significantly lower fees than actively managed funds, making them the lesser of two evils financially, they also contain too many securities for an investor to scrutinize. The intrinsic size and scale of mutual funds, and especially index funds and ETFs, makes comprehension, let alone management, futile for investors, fund managers, and directors.

Willard Libby didn't buy mutual funds, nor did he try

to re-create them on his own. He didn't own stock in more than ten or so companies at one time. He recognized that to hold stock in twenty—let alone two hundred—would make his portfolio unknowable, unmanageable, and almost certainly unprofitable.

Money Managers Gone Wild

The corporate leadership of a mutual fund complex or family controls the nomination of its board of directors. As a result, every director ultimately owes his or her job to the managers he or she is charged with overseeing. Ironically, the directors are legally obligated to monitor potential conflicts of interest.

The board determines director salaries, which are taken directly out of shareholder assets. *SmartMoney* reported that the typical director workload consists of attending between four and eight multiday board meetings a year; for this each director is paid $260,000 annually on average at the largest mutual fund families. In the article, former SEC chairman Arthur Levitt characterized mutual fund board membership as "the most comfortable position in corporate America."[18]

If the New York Yankees directly paid the salary of the referees presiding over their games, would the Red Sox call foul? Of course! The game would be fundamentally rigged, with bias tainting every call. Unfortunately, mutual fund shareholders have no real forum in which to call foul. And this fundamental conflict of interest pervades and subverts mutual funds' efforts around accountability. "The real puzzle isn't why these safeguards don't work," University of Virginia Law School professor John Morley, an expert on this issue, told *SmartMoney*. "It's why anybody thinks they could work."[19]

Past Performance and Future Results

In a market with more than seven thousand options,[20] how do inexperienced investors—the target market for mutual funds—choose which ones to buy? Studies have shown that investors often make whimsical decisions about the funds they buy and sell, and that fund names can be a major factor.[21] This is the rough equivalent of purchasing a house, sight unseen, because of the name of the street it's on.

Mutual funds typically market themselves on the basis of having amassed a successful track record (see Figure 9). This naturally leads some investors to buy shares in funds that have delivered strong returns in the past. To encourage this kind of "performance chasing," mutual funds promote the "ratings" awarded to them by third-party analyst firms such as Morningstar and Lipper (see Figure 10).

Undermining all the research and ratings, however, is the inescapable fact that previous success is not a reliable predictor of future achievement. No one can consistently predict what markets will do, or how funds will perform, in the future. After periods of great financial success, companies such as Research in Motion, Lehman Brothers, and AIG lost billions of dollars of their investors' money. No company is immune to decline, and the fortunes of a "conservative investment" can change overnight.

In an interview for this book, Jack Bogle said it best: "If you pore slavishly over the past numbers, it will tell you a lot about the past—but nothing about the future."

Of course, mutual funds are legally required to acknowledge this in their communication. As a result, some variation of the industry's oracular axiom—"past performance is

Hypothetical Growth of $10,000

AS OF 12/31/2014; MORNINGSTAR CATEGORY: LARGE GROWTH

■ Fidelity® Growth Discovery Fund ☑ ‖ Russell 3000 Growth   ☑ ‖ S&P 500/R3000G
☑ ‖ Large Growth

Compare Chart | Fund Facts Search

The performance data featured represents past performance, which is no guarantee of future results. Investment return and principal value of an investment will fluctuate; therefore, you may have a gain or loss when you sell your shares. Current performance may be higher or lower than the performance data quoted.

Figure 9. Fidelity Growth Discovery Fund, Performance and Risk

Fidelity® Magellan® Fund

Buy/Trade

FMAGX | NTF No Transaction Fee [1] | 🏆 Fidelity Fund Pick

Add to Watch List | Compare

Summary | Performance & Risk | **Ratings** | Composition | Fees and Distributions | Commentary | View All Tabs

Morningstar Ratings ❷

AS OF 12/31/2014; MORNINGSTAR CATEGORY: LARGE GROWTH

Overall	★★☆☆☆	Out of **1,528 funds**
3 Yr	★★★★★	Out of **1,528 funds**
5 Yr	★★☆☆☆	Out of **1,324 funds**
10 Yr	★☆☆☆☆	Out of **909 funds**

An overall rating for a fund is derived from a weighted average of the performance figures associated with its 3-, 5- and 10-year (if applicable) Morningstar Metrics as of the date stated. The number of funds in the Large Growth category tracked by Morningstar was 1528 for the 3 year period and Overall Ranking; 1324 for the 5 year period; and 909 for the 10 year period. Please click on the question mark above for additional Morningstar information.

Past performance is no guarantee of future results.

Figure 10. Ratings for Fidelity Magellan Fund, 2014

no guarantee of future results"—can be found in every mutual fund prospectus and marketing pamphlet and on every fund website (see Figure 11).

Performance

The following information is intended to help you understand the risks of invest-ing in the fund. The information illus-trates the changes in the performance of the fund's shares from year to year and compares the performance of the fund's shares to the performance of a securities market index and an addi-tional index over various periods of time. The indexes have characteristics relevant to the fund's investment strate-gies. Index descriptions appear in the Additional Index Information section of the prospectus. Prior to February 1, 2007, the fund operated under certain different investment policies and com-pared its performance to a different in-dex. The fund's historical performance may not represent its current invest-ment policies. Past performance (before and after taxes) is not an indication of future performance.

Figure 11. Excerpt from Fidelity International Capital Appreciation Fund Summary Prospectus

And so, it is widely acknowledged, even within the industry, that prior performance has no bearing on future performance. Yet, historic performance remains the primary factor in many financial analysts' fund ratings, which are often marketed as suggestive of future potential by the funds themselves. Despite this fallacy, year after year, investors pour money into highly rated funds, even though analyst firms warn (usually in fine print) that "a high rating alone is not a sufficient basis for investment decisions."

This key fact bears repeating: prior performance has no bearing on future performance.

Death, Taxes, and Fees

No investor knows how a particular mutual fund will perform in the future. But, like death and taxes, mutual fund fees are both predictable and inescapable. The industry has intentionally obscured its methodologies for charging fees by calling them by other names and using obscure financial equations to calculate them. This strategy has worked beautifully, deterring all but the most committed and masochistic investors from even attempting to comprehend the cost of their investments.

The research bears this out. According to survey results published by Charles Schwab, only 21 percent of "highly engaged" investors have discussed fees in detail with their investment adviser. In contrast, 83 percent of respondents in the study said they examine the ingredients before buying food. Less than 20 percent reviewed how fees and commissions impacted their returns, yet nearly 70 percent have called a company to better understand a bill. Only 12 percent had a detailed conversation about how their investment adviser was compensated, but more than two-thirds had called a phone, cable, or other service provider to ask about better service or lower rates.[22]

Nevertheless, if you can bear to wade through a prospectus, you'll learn that you can't do much with a mutual fund—including buy, sell, exchange, or even "maintain" one—without incurring a fee. These charges are numerous in type and often comically dubious in their derivation. But they add up.

An Overview of Common Mutual Fund Fees

Funds often pay brokers and financial advisers to sell shares to investors. These payments, known as distribution fees or 12b-1 fees, come directly out of fund assets—and they aren't always disclosed. Just because you don't see them listed explicitly on your monthly statement doesn't mean you're not being charged.

Brokers may charge other fees, which are typically referred to as "loads" (without any apparent irony). There are many types of loads, each associated with a different mutual fund share class. Though every share class is invested identically, there are distinctions among their fee and expense structures.[23]

Class A shares have a front-end load. Investors pay this fee to brokers to buy into a fund. In this context, a $10,000 purchase of Class A shares in a fund with a 1 percent front-end sales load would actually net a customer only $9,900 in shares, minus the $100 payment to the broker. It's kind of like buying a pizza and having the guy at the counter take a slice out of the box and eat it in front of you.

Regulations require mutual funds to disclose the fees they charge in the fund prospectus. Of course, when investors buy shares through a broker or financial adviser, there may be fees that are not disclosed in the prospectus.[24] Some charge fees when investors exchange or sell shares. Others may charge fees to cover "basic operational costs," such as investment advisory services, brokerage transactions, and custodial, legal, and accounting expenses.

Understandably, as investors learn more about the impact of fees on returns, mutual fund companies are adjusting their language and introducing new lines of *no-load funds*. No-load funds have soared in popularity over the past ten years, and accounted for roughly two-thirds of total long-term fund assets in 2013, compared to less than half in 2003.[25] This seems to suggest that some investors are, in fact, paying attention. Perhaps many really do comprehend the fees being charged.

But no-load funds still charge fees. They just call them by other names.

A no-load fund may still charge *exchange fees* for transferring assets to another fund within the same fund group. They may charge *account fees* for "maintenance" or when an account balance falls below a certain threshold. They may charge *purchase fees* in addition to front-end sales loads.

The increasing demand for no-load funds reflects the dawning awareness among some investors. And yet the vast majority of them remain mystified by the great financial shell game.

Because Willard Libby didn't buy mutual funds, he didn't have to pay these fees. Any returns accrued to him. There was no middleman taking a cut.

The Ugly Math

Mutual funds' failure to clearly and comprehensively disclose the fees they charge is one half of the ethical story; the financial impact of fees is the other. Fees can have an

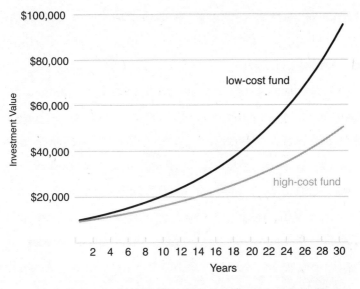

Both funds assume an initial $10,000 investment and 8% annual growth over 30 years.
Source: Bogleheads.org

Figure 12. Investment Growth of Low-Cost Fund vs. High-Cost Fund

extraordinary effect on returns—both in the short run and over a lifetime (see Figure 12).

As the chart shows, a $10,000 investment over thirty years can deliver two very different returns depending on the fees. With no sales loads and expenses of 0.2 percent per year, the value of the low-cost fund grows to $95,184. With an initial 5.75 percent sales load, expenses of 2.0 percent per year, and a 0.25 percent 12b-1 fee, the high-cost fund exacts from an investor 2.25 percent in fees every year. The net difference between the two—$44,753—is due entirely to fees.[26]

According to the Investment Company Institute, the typical actively managed stock-based mutual fund charges $74 per year on average for every $10,000 invested,[27] and it's not unheard of for actively managed funds to charge sales loads on top of these fees.[28] This represents an improvement from 2000, when the average cost was $99 per $10,000 invested, and suggests that the fund companies are beginning to feel some pressure from the ranks of awakened investors.

The irony is that studies show that high fees have no correlation with superior performance. In fact, a 2010 Morningstar study found that the mutual funds with the lowest fees consistently produced higher returns than the funds with the highest fees.[29] Of course, the cost of investing—the fees—is often just as important as market forces in determining an investor's net returns.

Mutual funds make an art of obscuring fees and their impact. Issues that are important to investors—how fees, inflation, and taxes impact returns, for example—are more or less ignored. More important, mutual fund fees underlie

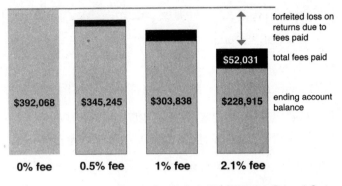

Figure 13. The Fee Effect

a basic conflict of interest: higher fees mean higher profits for fund managers and lower returns for shareholders (see Figure 13).

Fees Stack Up

- According to the SEC, a $10,000 investment in a fund that produced a 10 percent annual return before expenses and that charges shareholders 1.5 percent in fees to cover operating expenses would produce a return of $49,725 after twenty years; in contrast, a 0.5 percent fee would produce a return of $60,858 in the same period.[30]

- According to the Department of Labor, a 1 percent difference in fees and expenses can reduce an account balance by up to 28 percent over thirty-five years (assuming an average return of 7 percent). On a $25,000 investment, that would result in a forfeiture of $64,000.[31]

- Data provided to the authors by the Bogle Financial Markets Research Center show that the average annual stock market return from 1983 to 2011 was 10.3 percent compared to an average mutual equity fund return of 8.2 percent, with the difference due primarily to fees. On an initial investment of $25,000, an annual 2.1 percent fee would reduce an account balance by $163,152 over twenty-eight years.

It's no surprise, then, that the average mutual fund investor's return was about 40 percent lower than the stock market's overall return from 1983 to 2011.[32] Still, in a testament to the mutual fund industry's combination of omnipresence and potent marketing, roughly 80 percent of mutual fund shareholders were "confident in mutual funds' ability to help them achieve their financial goals."[33]

It must be mentioned that some index funds and ETFs have lowered fees to a truly nominal level; Vanguard, Schwab, and others offer funds that charge investors $1 in management fees for every $1,000 invested; these funds are also highly accessible, available with a minimum investment of $100. Though index funds and ETFs mitigate some of the financial drawbacks of actively managed funds, they contain, by definition, too many securities for an investor to comprehend.

Still, James Kaplan, who serves on the board of an investment analysis firm, suggests that investors have learned to accept high fees and lousy returns. In an interview for this book, he said, "People have been taught to have lower expectations, they've been dumbed down, and they think that's a fair and reasonable expectation for their capital at risk."

Pay and Performance Disconnected

When it comes to money managers, compensation has little to do with performance. Fund managers are paid a percentage of the assets they manage. This naturally encourages fund managers to focus on increasing their assets under management rather than investor returns. The bigger the pool of money, the more the managers make, while the mission of earning returns for investors is subordinated.

"These houses that are running money for individuals and institutions—they are just asset gatherers," said investment manager Stewart Gardner in an interview for this book. "[A very large investment or wealth management firm's performance] doesn't matter for the most part, unless you're a hedge fund. You've got a trillion under management, you're collecting billions in fees."

Indeed, fund managers make money whether they win or lose. Investors pay fees no matter what. This model has its roots in poorly designed regulations that distort the investor–financial adviser relationship with misguided incentives.

Remarkably, one of the most significant laws governing today's financial industry was passed more than seventy years ago. The Investment Advisers Act of 1940 forbids investment advisers from being compensated "based on a share of capital gains on, or capital appreciation of, the funds of a client."[34] This statute effectively prohibits investors from rewarding their money managers for investing their capital successfully. The rationale is that paying them based on the returns they generate would encourage irresponsible risk taking in order to maximize pay.[35]

Congress has exempted high-net-worth individuals and institutional investors from the Investment Advisers Act's compensation provisions, however. The "performance fee" restriction leaves a loophole for "persons that the Commission determines do not need the protections"—that is, high-net-worth individuals and institutions—"who are financially experienced and able to bear the risks of performance fee arrangements."[36] This is why direct access to private equity and hedge funds is generally restricted to wealthy clients.

But many of us are stuck paying mutual fund managers regardless of how well they perform. It's a striking contrast to other, more direct forms of investment. When you develop real estate, for example, you and your investors make money only if the project succeeds. When you invest in a startup, you lose your money if it fails. When you buy stock, your investment is tethered to success of the company. In Latin, this is called *bonus* (reward) and *malus* (punishment).

For a mutual fund manager, however, it's all bonus. What happens when you buy shares of a mutual fund that hemorrhages money? Does the fund manager apologize? Beg for forgiveness? Offer a refund? Of course not! The fund manager gently reminds you that picking stocks is a risky business and commiserates with you about the "market environment." And that fund continues to gobble up fees, passing them on to executives through salaries and bonuses, whether or not it ever makes money for clients.

Fund managers' compensation is the financial equivalent of contemporary Little League culture, in which every player receives an award just for participating. It's a corrupt system, rife with moral hazards, distorted incentives, and fuel for poor corporate decision making.

Willard Libby bought stocks. There were no performance fees. When his stocks went up, Willard made money. When his stocks went down, Willard lost money. The mutuality of this arrangement made Willard and the companies in which he invested equal partners. He supported those companies with his capital and shared in their fortunes.

No Skin in the Game

Common sense suggests that mutual funds would perform better when fund managers have a significant amount of their own money invested in them. Most investors would certainly welcome this additional comfort. According to an article in *U.S. News & World Report,* "Morningstar found a correlation between portfolio managers' investment in their funds and fund performance."[37]

A study by the Capital Group echoed this finding, and a *Financial Times* article about it (as well as other studies) reports, "if you only pick funds from companies whose managers have the most skin in the game, you substantially improve your odds of beating the market."[38] That noted, it's not always easy to figure out whether or not a manager has actually invested in his or her own fund. But Russel Kinnel, Morningstar's head of mutual fund research, suggests that only a minority actually do so. "There are hundreds of funds where a manager has millions invested, but there are thousands of funds where they don't invest anything."[39]

Putting your money where your mouth is not only looks good—it goes a long way toward mitigating conflicts of interest. No investors want their money manager to take huge risks with their money that he wouldn't take with his own.

Investing in One Dimension

Third-party analysts, such as Morningstar, credit-rating agencies, traditional accounting firms, and the financial media, have trained investors to consider their investments in exclusively financial terms. Mutual funds, in particular, encourage this one-dimensional perspective. Because funds and pundits are most comfortable with conventional metrics such as earnings per share, market capitalization, and quarterly returns, they emphasize these topics in their assessments. The success of an investment is nearly always measured by its return.

This highlights one of the major sacrifices one makes by investing in mutual funds and underscores a major missed opportunity for many kinds of investors. Though the financial component of investing is critically important, invested capital can also be a powerful way to influence social, environmental, and economic issues that are important to you.

Investment must be seen as an *endorsement* of a corporation's practices, activities, and values. Investing in a company is like voting with your dollars. Doesn't it make sense to support the companies, products, and services that you like and believe in? And to withhold your capital from corporations that you don't like or believe in?

Mainstream mutual funds make selective, values-based investing nearly impossible, given their typical blanket approach. There is, however, a small and growing subset of funds that do acknowledge issues-based investing; the number of "socially responsible investing" vehicles increased from 55 in 1995 to 493 in 2012.[40] Still, these types of funds account for a relatively modest share of the market overall, and they don't resolve many other issues inherent in mutual fund investing.

Funds require a transactional type of investing: an investor's involvement begins with handing over her money and ends with a quarterly statement. Though mutual fund investors have been trained to stand on the sidelines, their money connects them to hundreds of companies and makes them complicit, consciously or not, in their activities.

The most rewarding (and financially productive) investments offer investors the opportunity to open a dialogue, exert influence, and express an opinion. When you buy a share of stock, for example, your investment entitles you to

attend the company's annual meeting and vote on important corporate issues such as executive compensation and
who sits on the company's board of directors.

If you can't attend the meeting in person (few investors
do), you can vote by proxy—sort of like absentee voting in
a political election. This *proxy voting* is a major opportunity for investors to advance their own agendas and influence the decision making within corporations in which
they've invested.

The potential of this mechanism for influencing corporate behavior remains largely untapped, however. There is
a critical difference between owning stock outright and
"owning" a stock through a mutual fund. When you buy a
stock outright, you are eligible to vote your proxy. When you
buy into a mutual fund, you are not. While the vast majority of stock is "owned" through mutual funds, the fund
managers vote on the investors' behalf—usually without
their input—on corporate issues with social, environmental, political, and financial implications.

Though some funds may solicit opinions from their
shareholders on proxy issues, ultimately fund managers have
full discretion over the vote. When you buy into a mutual
fund, you surrender your vote and your voice.

As the holders of a significant share of US corporate

stock, mutual funds (and other large institutional investors such as hedge funds and pension funds) are legally required to vote their proxies. With their immense wealth and capacity to consolidate the power of a vast but dispersed body of shareholders, they have the potential to remedy many contemporary corporate issues such as exorbitant CEO salaries.

Unfortunately, year after year, fund managers vote with corporate managers. In 2013, the AFL-CIO published an examination of votes cast by the largest mutual fund families to constrain CEO pay. The median level of mutual fund opposition to executive compensation was only 10 percent.[41] Given that fund managers collect fees and commissions regardless of their portfolio's performance, they have few incentives to intervene on investors' behalf in matters of executive compensation or anything else.

"When you look at the profile of an S&P 500 company, you see that the institutional ownership is 60 or 70 or 75 percent," said Jamie Heard, an investor and corporate governance expert, in an interview for this book. "Then you go down the list and you see who the owners are. They're all fund managers. Mutual funds have the power to hold managements and boards accountable if they want to exercise that power."

"I've had investment managers tell me they don't care if

management is fraudulent as long as they make money," says Jim Kaplan, a corporate governance and forensic accounting expert who also serves on the board of an investment analysis firm. "It's absolutely organizational, cultural. I can't tell you that at the very top there's a policy: they don't want to deal with fraud, but they're indifferent. In reality, the amount of energy they had to put into the process was more than they were willing to commit. They are not making fiduciary decisions on behalf of their clients—they are making business decisions."

The *New York Times* reports that the median compensation for CEOs in 2013 was $13.9 million, a 9 percent increase from 2012.[42] Though Dodd-Frank officially granted US shareholders the opportunity to hold an advisory vote on executive pay packages in 2012, as of June 2013, 98 percent of these "say-on-pay" proposals have been approved.[43] The data show that mutual funds (and other institutional money managers) agree that multimillion-dollar compensation packages accurately reflect shareholders' values and expectations.

The SEC may soon require companies to publish a ratio comparing a chief executive's pay to the median pay of the company's employees.[44] Though CEO compensation is only the most conspicuous evidence of mutual funds' failure to protect the interests of investors, it is instructive of fund

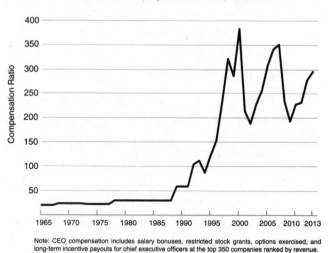

CEO-to-Worker Compensation Ratio, 1965–2013

Note: CEO compensation includes salary bonuses, restricted stock grants, options exercised, and long-term incentive payouts for chief executive officers at the top 350 companies ranked by revenue.

Source: Economic Policy Institute

managers' unwillingness to represent shareholder interests in less visible matters of operations and governance.

In the mutual fund business, and indeed the financial sector overall, the fox has been left to guard the henhouse. It's the textbook definition of an "agency problem," wherein agents (the funds) have incentives that are not aligned with those who have hired them (shareholders).

We discussed this issue with Jack Bogle. He said, "The corporate managers are not representing their shareholders adequately, and the money managers are not representing their pension beneficiaries and mutual fund holders adequately. All

these agents are putting their own interest first—and that's how you get the happy conspiracy. They both like stock prices better than stock values. They both like the evanescent better than the enduring."

———

Exorbitant CEO salaries benefit no one but the CEOs and their families. The governance structures pervasive among mutual funds and corporations foster a distorted culture that pits executives' interests against those of the shareholders that ultimately own their companies.

5

No Escape from the Big Sleep

Mutual funds have become a central component of contemporary mainstream investing and retirement planning. They also neatly embody just about every hazard investors will encounter in the market.

Though they are among the largest institutional investors in the financial sector, they are not the only players in the game. In fact, their problems, conflicts, and inequities can be found in nearly every part of the money management industry. In many ways, the flaws of mutual funds are the flaws of the financial sector writ large.

There are trillions of dollars in the hands of trust companies, registered investment advisers, private equity firms, hedge funds, and pension funds. As with mutual funds, each of these subjects investors to conflicts of interest, massive complexity, high fees, and minimal opportunities for accountability. Regardless of portfolio size, asset class, or investment type, investors have few safe harbors from the unseemly practices of the modern financial industrial complex.

Hedge Funds: High Fees and Low Returns for the Luxury Class

The investment vehicle du jour for wealthy individuals and institutional investors, hedge funds had more than $2.5 trillion under management in early 2014.[1] Despite a reputation for impossibly complex financial wizardry, the business of hedge funds is pretty straightforward. Like mutual funds, they are actively managed investment portfolios. Though their name suggests they're designed to reduce risk—known colloquially as "hedging"—most hedge funds focus on maximizing returns. In fact, because they often traffic in highly speculative investments, investing in hedge funds can be far riskier than dealing with other market players.

That there is no exact legal definition for *hedge fund* is indicative of the variety of things these investment groups do to make to money. This is a key difference from mutual funds, which are fairly limited in terms of the equities they can trade and tactics they can use. Another important distinction is that hedge funds are directly accessible only to wealthy investors: individuals and organizations such as pension funds, mutual funds, and other hedge funds with a net worth of at least $1 million.[2]

Hedge funds have exponentially more options when it comes to investing than mutual funds. They can take long and short positions, concentrate investments (instead of diversifying), use leverage, invest in illiquid assets, trade derivatives, and hold unlisted securities. Still, most invest in the same securities available to mutual funds and individual investors.[3]

With a well-heeled clientele, hedge funds can charge high fees. The standard arrangement, known colloquially as "two and twenty," features a management fee of 2 percent, which the fund collects simply for managing the money. There is also often an incentive fee that entitles the fund to pocket 20 percent (or more) of any returns it generates with an investor's capital above some threshold. So, it's not a bad business to be in.

There is also a subset of hedge funds called *funds of hedge funds*. Nothing more complicated than a collection of hedge funds, these financial instruments generally have lower minimum investment requirements than a traditional

hedge fund. Despite the fact that funds of hedge funds subject investors to yet another layer of management and performance fees on top of fees exacted by the underlying funds, funds of hedge funds are increasingly popular and now represent roughly one-quarter of the assets invested in the hedge fund market.[4]

Hedge funds are extremely opaque and have no obligations to disclose details about fund management, holdings, fees, expenses, or performance. They are not required to maintain any level of liquidity. They are not compelled to make shares easily redeemable. They are not required to protect investors from conflicts of interest or even to price shares "fairly."

In short, hedge funds prove that wealthy investors are just as vulnerable to financial mismanagement as the rest of us. In an interview for this book, hedge fund manager Gareth Shepherd observed, "It's fascinating to see how badly served [wealthy clients] are and how many stupid products are out there that people are trying to shove down their throats."

The data back this up. A December 2012 *Economist* article, "Going Nowhere Fast," reports that the S&P 500 outperformed the hedge fund market for a decade—except in 2008, when both suffered dramatic losses: "A simple-minded investment portfolio, 60 percent of it in [stock] shares and the rest in sovereign bonds, has delivered returns of more than 90 percent over the last decade, compared with a meager 17 percent after fees for hedge funds."[5] In 2012, a Reuters article corroborated this finding: "This is the state of the hedge fund industry in 2012: The most profitable [hedge] fund in the world underperformed a simple S&P index fund."[6] And in 2013, Bloomberg reported that "hedge funds trailed the Standard & Poor's 500 Index for the fifth straight year."[7]

There are some appealing things about hedge funds. Managers often make significant personal investments in their own funds. And, of course, some funds consistently deliver superior returns. Generally, these are the funds with managers actively involved in their investments, who communicate clearly and straightforwardly with their investors. But they are few and far between.

Pension Funds: Another Pawn in the Game

Despite their recent declines, pension funds remain a key institutional investor, controlling assets earmarked to fund the retirements of millions of beneficiaries. According to Towers Watson, the top twenty US pension funds controlled more than $2 trillion in assets at the end of 2013.[8]

In contrast to mutual fund shareholders, private-sector pension beneficiaries are protected by the Employee Retirement Income Security Act of 1974, which requires greater financial disclosure and upholds stronger standards of conduct for plan fiduciaries. Beneficiaries are also protected by the Pension Benefit Guaranty Corporation (PBGC) in the event that their pension plans fail, though the program is said to have a multibillion-dollar deficit, according to the *New York Times*.[9] (Note that the PBGC generally does not provide insurance for defined contribution plans.)[10]

Still, pension funds often hire fund managers, which subjects them to many of the same fees as mutual fund investors. Typically, trustees and executives, after being advised by an investment consultant, who charges a fee, allocate pension assets to fund managers, who charge additional fees and in turn distribute the monies to other asset managers, who charge more fees. In addition, external fund and asset managers may have different incentives, such as increasing assets under management or trading securities more often than is necessary to collect fees, in conflict with beneficiaries' objectives.

In many ways, pension beneficiaries are even more disenfranchised than mutual fund investors. In the case of defined benefit plans, participants do not even have the option to divest; investment is a requirement. Though some public pension funds, such as the California Public Employees' Retirement System (CalPERS), actively intervene in fund and corporate governance on behalf of investors, they do so at their own discretion. Beneficiaries are no more able to influence their investments than mutual fund investors.

Taking the Best, Leaving the Rest

Of course, there are some mainstream approaches to investing that have redeeming qualities. The *private equity* model, for example, can be an efficient way to collect and deploy capital to companies to help them grow while earning worthwhile returns for investors.

Venture capital, a subcategory of private equity, typically makes smaller investments in early-stage start-up companies, which can be valuable and lucrative for investors, the companies and their employees, and the economy overall. Traditional private equity funds tend to invest in mature companies that need cash to grow.

In both cases, the managers raising the money usually invest their own capital along with money raised from others. This can do wonders in aligning the incentives of investors, fund managers, and businesses—everyone is in it together.

Private equity investors are by and large active, engaged groups or individuals who tend to cultivate simple, straight lines of accountability between themselves and business managers. In my experience, having owners "in the shop" usually results in better decision making. At the minimum, it increases the opportunities for executives, who may be otherwise insulated from direct feedback, to receive constructive criticism.

In an interview for this book with private equity manager Mark Colodny, he discussed the benefits of having the owner "in the shop":

> *The way we function is all about accountability. We're quite active. Having very engaged board members who spend a lot of time studying the performance, meeting with management, in some cases*

talking to other competitors in the marketplace to understand what's going on, is a pretty powerful check for private companies with private equity ownership. The public shareholders can't do that. In theory, the way that this was supposed to work was that the board is supposed to act as a proxy for the shareholders who couldn't be present. If the board doesn't do its job and isn't paying attention or has incentives not to, then, as you say, there is no owner in the shop.

Private equity is not without its flaws, however. It subjects investors to the same types of fees favored by hedge funds, in which investors pay 2 percent of the amount of assets they have under management as well as 20 percent of returns above a certain threshold. Sometimes the pressure to deliver high returns drives private equity investors to pressure managers to focus on the short term at the expense of the long term. Private equity funds also have a history of taking on irresponsible amounts of leverage (borrowing capital to increase potential returns), a practice that can harm investors as well as portfolio companies and their employees when investments don't pan out.

In addition, direct private equity investments are generally restricted to high-net-worth individuals and organizations. As a result, one of the few models that offer investors a more equitable share of profits, a more mutual partnership, and the opportunity for a higher level of engagement is available only to the very wealthy.

The Cross-Pollination of High Finance

Institutional investors, including private equity funds, public pension funds, and endowments, invest huge sums of their clients' money in hedge funds and mutual funds. Given this, investors are increasingly unable to escape the fees, conflicts of interest, and other drawbacks endemic to these collective investment models. The lesson: regardless of where you outsource your money, it inevitably ends up feeding a monolithic financial industrial complex.

In 2000, the managers of CalPERS, the country's largest public pension fund, committed $1 billion of direct investment to hedge funds. It took the organization fourteen years (and millions in fees) to tire of the arrangement, but at last, in September 2014, CalPERS announced that it would wind down its $4.5 billion hedge fund portfolio to "reduce complexity and costs." This came after the fund

spent roughly $250 million in hedge fund fees in just the previous two years.[11] And yet, as reported by the *New York Times*, CalPERS's hedge fund portfolio and corresponding fees were minute compared with its $31 billion private equity fund program, on which it spent $476 million in fees in 2013 alone.[12]

Despite hedge funds' unappealing combination of persistently high fees and uneven returns, pension funds are increasingly hungry to invest in them. According to a recent survey published by J.P. Morgan, 46 percent of pension funds increased the percentage of their portfolio dedicated to hedge fund investment in 2013, and half expected to increase this percentage in 2014.[13] Hedge fund managers will surely welcome the business.

Mutual funds are finding new ways to get into this lucrative market as well. In August 2013, Fidelity opened access to the Blackstone Alternative Multi-Manager Fund to some investors. With a minimum investment of $2,500, the fund gives mutual fund investors exposure to an assortment of hedge funds. As of April 2015, it carried a 2.68 percent net expense ratio.[14] Mash-ups like these make it more difficult for investors to proactively avoid the pitfalls of any given investment type.

Despite the real differences, significant and superficial, among the various investment classes, a similar set of problems undermines them all. Regardless of the point of entry, investors' capital ends up in the same system, subject to the same drawbacks.

6

Awakened:
A Better Way to Invest

Now the good news.

There is a better way to invest—a simpler, more sustainable way. It requires only that investors, individually and collectively, take back what is rightfully theirs: control over and responsibility for their investing.

This better way is not necessarily an easier way to invest. It is not a shortcut. And it offers no guarantee of untold riches tomorrow or next year. (But, of course, no one can honestly make that guarantee.)

This better way to invest does not require a massive expenditure of time, effort, or intellect. You need not become a full-time day trader. You need not go back to school for an MBA. You need not be Albert Einstein, Warren Buffett, or Gordon Gekko.

This better way requires only an investor's attention, willingness to take responsibility, and commitment to getting a fair shake.

This better way requires an investor to be invested.

Willard's Way

Willard Libby's do-it-yourself approach remains the most cost-efficient, ethical, and prudent way to invest. Investors who are informed, engaged, and hands-on have the best chance of earning great returns. They avoid surrendering significant portions of their financial gains in fees to middlemen. They support the companies in which they believe, and they hold these companies accountable. They make their voices heard, and they take responsibility for the implications of their investments.

Willard Libby was invested. He did his homework. He read financial statements. He bought stock in companies in which he believed, in businesses that made sense to him. If he didn't understand the business, he didn't invest. He didn't make investments unconsciously. He didn't invest in companies that ran counter to his values. He recognized brokers for what they were (and are): salespeople.

Willard avoided mutual funds and other financial products that came attached to complicated fees or nebulous commissions. His returns were tied up in the long-term performances of companies he had handpicked, and he invested in no more than ten or so at a time. He recognized that holding too many investments at once would make his portfolio unknowable, unmanageable, and almost certainly unprofitable. If Willard owned stock in a company that was engaged in an activity or strategy that didn't make sense to him, he expressed his opinion directly; he voted his proxy. Or he sent a message, albeit a relatively small one, by divesting.

Imagine the power of a million Willards! They could change the world. We recognize that most people feel unequipped to invest on their own; the modern financial industry has been designed and built to exploit their discomfort. And there are still plenty of valid reasons to seek out the counsel and support of a financial adviser or professional money manager.

Yet the problem remains: the current system does not support the ethical treatment of investors.

Though Willard is the paragon, it's unrealistic to expect that we should all invest in the way he did.

So, as we work to empower investors, encouraging them to take the reins themselves, with a group of partners, I am also actively building and cultivating a new alternative to the modern financial industrial complex.

The Cooperative Investment Partnership

For the truly invested, we have envisioned an optimal money management arrangement. The *cooperative investment partnership* (CIP) is a hybrid, borrowing the best organizational qualities and financial practices from an array of entities while mitigating the flaws that are so prevalent across the investment landscape.

Like an open-source computer project, in which developers make their code free and accessible to anyone, this book presents our vision of the ideal ethical, organizational, and financial configuration for managing money. While we invite existing financial corporations to adopt the principles described below, we are not waiting for them.

We are exploring the best approach for incorporating a CIP ourselves to accommodate the growing population of dissatisfied investors.

We believe that once investors have the opportunity to choose a real alternative to the options currently on offer by the financial industrial complex, they will do so in numbers. Over time, this will force traditional money managers to follow or die.

The Blueprint: Eight Principles for Better Investing

The CIP draws heavily on the model of the *mutual corporation*, an organizational configuration that has been around for hundreds of years but that is now most common in the insurance and credit union businesses. Mutual corporations make customers co-owners of their business, giving them rights to share in profits and governance; these companies are not publicly traded and have no shareholders.

A mutual insurance company's profit is redistributed to its policyholders through dividends or reduced premiums.

Policyholders reap the benefits alongside employees and corporate executives. Everybody wins.

While serving on the board of the Maine Employers' Mutual Insurance Company (MEMIC), a private mutual company that facilitates workers' compensation insurance, I observed firsthand the power of a business and its customers sharing risk and reward. With a stated mission of reducing injuries, controlling costs, and improving work conditions, MEMIC was capitalized by its own customers, who were also co-owners of the venture and entitled to share in profits and have board representation. Over time, MEMIC reduced lost-time injuries in Maine by 30 percent and issued dividends and a capital return of more than $146 million.[1]

1. Profit Sharing. Redistribution of profits is the cornerstone of the CIP model. The concept is simple: the company's net profits, earned through management and administrative fees collected from investors, are redistributed proportionally back to those investors on an annual basis. This ultimately reduces the cost of investing for investors. Note that the profit-sharing mechanism involves fees only and is wholly separate and distinct from returns or losses associated with a CIP client's investment portfolio.

2. Skin in the Game. Taking a page from hedge funds and private equity firms, CIP money managers are required to have their own skin in the game—that is, to invest a significant amount of their own money alongside their investors. This mitigates a currently pervasive conflict of interest: money managers taking outsize risks with other people's money instead of their own.

This practice is extended throughout the organization, and a percentage of every CIP employee's compensation is allocated to a company fund that receives its own proportional share of profits. With their own money invested in the CIP, every employee has an integral stake in the business; this increases the likelihood that every element of the business is treated with diligence, care, and thoughtfulness. It also ensures basic equality: if owners and employees win, so do customers.

3. Clear Communication. The CIP provides investors with clear, timely financial statements that include details about its revenue, expenses, and profits.

4. Proxy Voting. The CIP encourages its investors to vote their proxy at every opportunity and accommodates this by providing online analysis and voting tools.

5. Insourcing. The CIP does not outsource financial expertise. Instead of paying fees to external entities such as hedge funds or real estate funds, the organization has board directors who are also investors in the CIP. These directors are required to have relevant domain experience to help guide the CIP managers' investment strategy. This not only makes the CIP smarter and stronger, focusing its investments on areas it knows best, it eliminates the need to pay fees to outside intermediaries and money managers who aren't personally invested in the CIP portfolio.

6. Fair Pay. The CIP mitigates inequality by capping compensation for top executives at ten times the company's median salary; this both creates greater equity among employees and increases the likelihood that the majority of profits are redistributed back to investors.

The CIP also tethers pay to performance, integrating *bonus* and *malus* into every employee's compensation. CIP money managers are paid, in part, according to how well they perform over a defined period of time; if they fail to deliver a specified return, their compensation reflects that failure. Again, CIP managers invest their own money alongside customers, so if the customers lose, managers lose, too.

7. Informational Integrity. Because conventional accounting and rating agencies have been thoroughly compromised, there is an untapped demand for reliable information to inform investment decisions. CIPs purchase information only from companies that provide independent, conflict-free analyses of corporate financial, environmental, and governance activities.

8. Indication of Intention. The typical corporate annual report provides only the narrowest picture of a public company's actual strengths, weaknesses, objectives, and conduct. And yet it's one of the key tools investors use to make investment decisions. Corporations should provide investors with a simpler and broader statement of their values and intentions.

A framework for this type of statement already exists. In New Zealand and Australia, disclosures like these are mandatory for some governmental agencies, public entities, and companies: their statements of corporate intent (SCIs) "publicly set out their intentions and activities for the forthcoming three years . . . [to] provide a basis for shareholders and the wider public to assess . . . performance."[2]

Published by a corporation's board of directors, an SCI

provides a comprehensive account of a company's activities and long-term vision, covering topics such as executive compensation and governance as well as environmental and social practices. It provides a more versatile benchmark for evaluating executive performance than today's strictly financial criteria. CIPs also support annual audits by independent parties to assess an SCI and measure a company's progress against its stated goals.

———

The CIP model is applicable to virtually any type of financial business—from mutual funds to private equity to hedge funds—regardless of strategy, risk tolerance, or asset class. The core conflicts of interests common to so many financial companies today are mitigated most effectively when investors are owners, and owners are investors.

We believe that financial advisers and money managers who *are* willing to shift to the new paradigm will instantly find a market of hungry investors eager to work with them. Some existing money managers, financial intermediaries, and big corporations will embrace this change. Most won't.

And they will be left behind.

7

Seven Ways to Reinvest

While the nascent cooperative investment partnership concept develops and matures, there is no shortage of things an investor can do today to take back ownership of and responsibility for his or her investing. Once an investor believes in the importance of building a more sustainable financial system, he or she can begin to help set new ground rules right now.

Here are seven important things all investors can do to reinvest:

1. Invest in Your Values

What you should know: Traditional factors such as time horizon, risk appetite, and asset allocation are important to consider, but so are values. If you're concerned about global warming, gun control, or genetically modified organisms in the food supply, you can put your money where your mouth is by investing in companies that reflect your position and avoiding those that don't.

What you can do: Analyze your portfolio and identify companies that reflect and uphold your values. Or have your money manager do the research. If a corporation doesn't publicize its stance on a particular issue, ask.

2. Know Your Money Manager

What you should know: There are many financial professionals who work hard for their clients and many more who work only to make money for themselves.

What you can do: Ask your money manager if he (or she) adheres to the fiduciary standard, which obligates him to put your financial interests ahead of his. Ask if the products he sells you are the best for your needs or simply most profitable for him. Ask whether he puts money into the same investments he sells to you. Ask if he makes money—and how much—whether or not he generates a return for clients.

3. Seek Out Conflict-Free Information

What you should know: There is a growing number of independent sources of information that go beyond the one-dimensional, conflicted, unreliable data and analyses published by credit-rating agencies and accounting firms.

What you can do: Learn where your money manager gets his information, and steer him toward sources such as the Global Impact Investing Ratings System,[1] MCSI Ratings,[2] and Gimme Credit.[3]

4. Know the Contents of Your Portfolio

What you should know: The companies in which you invest, and the companies that facilitate your investments, do things that impact the environment, politics, and society.

What you can do: Hold them accountable. Request a comprehensive list of the specific investments in your portfolio, and see whether your money manager can produce one. Ask why those particular investments were chosen on your behalf. Decide whether they reflect your goals and values.

5. Vote Your Proxy

What you should know: Corporate governance matters. If your portfolio includes publicly owned equities, your financial adviser or fund manager has the opportunity to vote on your behalf on critical corporate issues that may have far-reaching social, environmental, political, and financial implications.

What you can do: Vote your proxy; now that it can be done online, it's easy to do. If you own stocks directly, make your voice heard. If you own mutual funds or other indirect financial instruments, discuss proxy issues with your money manager, and encourage him or her to sponsor proxy primaries, during which investors can debate corporate issues and express their opinions before a proxy ballot is cast. The mechanics of proxy voting, and the banality of so many of the issues involved, can be overwhelming. Part of your money manager's job is to help you sort through which of them are important to you.

6. Add Up the Fees You Pay

What you should know: Money managers and financial firms often obscure the fees they charge when reporting returns. Some keep the trading fees they charge investors; some pay broker-dealers to trade stocks and bonds and then collect a kickback. Some money managers don't even keep track of all the fees they charge.

What you can do: Ask your money manager to list and explain all the fees, including transaction costs, they charge or pass on to you. (Most will have a hard time doing this.) Ask for an analysis of your returns, opportunity costs, and the effects of fees, inflation, and taxes on your invested capital. Ask how much money you would have if you liquidated your portfolio today (this is your real account balance).

7. Invest in a CIP

What you should know: Without the investor, there is no investing. Every investment arrangement should reflect this fact and respect the investor as partner and contributor of the underlying capital. There is a better way to invest.

What you can do: Ask your money manager to share his profits with you. Ask for access to your money manager's corporate financial statements. Ask to have fees waived when a return isn't produced. Ask to be recognized as a partner in the investing process.

Conclusion

I.
—

If you own a single share of stock, you are an investor. If you are enrolled in a 401(k) or retirement savings plan, you are an investor. If you own one share of a mutual fund, you are an investor. If you have money in a pension fund, hedge fund, or private equity fund, you are an investor.

Your investments make you a participant and partner, whether you know it or not, in the businesses and financial instruments in which your capital is invested.

And as an investor, you belong to the one and only group powerful enough to change the system.

In an interview for this book, Carl Icahn said, "Money is my army." Icahn's notion of the power of money reflects reality, and can be applied to all investors, regardless of portfolio size.

Capital is power. And investors own the capital.

II.
—

The entire financial system depends on investors' capital. But the prevailing model of money management—a business that ostensibly *serves* investors—treats its customer base with a remarkable lack of respect and fairness. Whether dealing within the context of a big-box financial corporation, five-star mutual fund, or cutting-edge hedge fund, investors run into the same issues over and over again. The dubious industry practices we've identified are not confined to a handful of bad actors. They are systemic problems.

They are business as usual.

The major issues we face did not develop overnight. They

are the result of a series of evolutionary steps taken over the course of decades. Business, technology, globalization, politics, demographics, and the changing nature of work and employment are some of the factors in play. Though there is much blame to go around, there is no one central villain.

And these issues transcend the high fees, inconsistent returns, exorbitant bonuses, and exploitative business models. In fact, the stakes couldn't be higher. They include the most pressing and intractable problems we face today, from increasing income inequality to climate change to water scarcity.

Our collective capital is the lifeblood of the corporations that have caused or contributed to these problems. And our continued investment in them is a tacit, if not explicit, endorsement of their activity.

But imagine if we could use our corporations to *solve* our momentous problems instead of adding to them.

Imagine if we could make corporations the engines of good.

It's up to investors to drive this change. No one else— no elected official, no regulator, no investigative journalist— can save us. It's up to us, the investors, to exert our influence, flex our muscular capital, and demand change from the companies in which we invest.

III.

The combination of awakened, engaged investors and the cooperative investment partnership resolves many root problems. It restores our sense of ownership and control. It offers us a more integral stake in the risks, benefits, and responsibilities of investing.

A relationship built on communication, fiduciary duty, a clear expression of personal values, aligned interests, equity, and accountability empowers everyone. Making financial relationships more transparent creates an environment for better decision making.

As Willard Libby did, every investor must make a conscious decision about how, when, where, why, and in whom to invest. Each decision has an impact that reverberates throughout the system. Each decision is important, reinforcing the status quo or driving change. Each decision sends a message. Each decision brings us closer to the reality of a healthier, more sustainable, more equitable economy— or sends us back to sleep, destined only to dream of that better reality.

Acknowledgments

The authors would like to acknowledge the following people.

For helping shape and refine our ideas: Jack Bogle, Mark Colodny, Richard Dorfman, Barney Frank, Stewart Gardner, Jamie Heard, Carl Icahn, Sandra Jaffee, James Kaplan, Greg Kesich, Lowell Libby, Roger Milliken, Jr., Robert A. G. Monks, Isabelle Mullen, Tony Payne, Arthur Rosenzweig, Stuart Schultz, Gareth Shepherd, David Weil, and Charlie Woodworth.

For helping assemble all of the editorial pieces: James Atlas, Carrie Cattabriga, Stephanie Frerich, Maria Gagliano, Hannah Kinisky, Jesse Maeshiro, Kristen Schwenger, Aaron Staples, and Adrian Zackheim.

And for supporting us through the process: Bonnie, Max, and Mariah; Amy, Emma, Milo, and Eric; and Chris and Oliver.

Notes

Chapter 1—An Investor's Dream: Ownership Outsourced

1. New York Stock Exchange website, "Timeline: Trading, Highlights," accessed January 7, 2015, http://www1.nyse .com/about/history/timeline_trading.html.

2. Art Swift, "Despite High Stock Prices, Half in U.S. Wary of Investing," Gallup, January 17, 2014, http://www .gallup.com/poll/166886/despite-high-stock-prices-half -wary-investing.aspx.

3. "Teresa Ghilarducci: Why the 401(k) Is a 'Failed Experiment,'" transcription of interview conducted for *Frontline*, "The Retirement Gamble," April 23, 2013, http://www.pbs.org/wgbh/pages/frontline/business -economy-financial-crisis/retirement-gamble/teresa -ghilarducci-why-the-401k-is-a-failed-experiment/.

4. IHS, "Three Top Economists Agree 2009 Worst Financial Crisis Since Great Depression; Risks Increase If Right Steps Are Not Taken," *Business Wire*, February 27, 2009, http://www.reuters.com/article/2009/02/27/idUS193520+27-Feb-2009+BW20090227.

5. JPMorgan & Chase Co., "JPMorgan Chase Reports Fourth-Quarter 2009 Net Income of $3.3 Billion, or $0.74 Per Share, on Revenue of $25.2 Billion," press release, January 15, 2010, http://investor.shareholder .com/jpmorganchase/releasedetail.cfm?ReleaseID= 437888. The reader may find humor in the fact that even the title of this press release is footnoted, so that the definition of revenue may be "clarified."

6. David Ellis, "JP Morgan's Dimon Scores $16M Bonus," CNN.com, February 5, 2010, http://money.cnn.com/ 2010/02/05/news/companies/dimon_chase_bonus/.

7. Bank of America, "Bank of America Announces 2009 Net Income of $6.3 Billion," press release, January 20, 2010, http://investor.bankofamerica.com/phoenix.zhtml ?c=71595&p=irol-newsArticle&ID=1376998#fbid= 8zWWOsp6-Ki.

8. Tomoeh Murakami Tse, "Bank of America CEO to Get No Salary for 2009," *Washington Post*, October 16,

2009, http://www.washingtonpost.com/wp-dyn/content/article/2009/10/15/AR2009101503929.html.

9. Wells Fargo & Company, *Wells Fargo & Company Annual Report 2009*, January 2010, https://www08.wellsfargomedia.com/downloads/pdf/invest_relations/wf2009annualreport.pdf.

10. E. Scott Reckard, "Wells Fargo CEO Is Highest-Paid Banker at $22.87 Million," *Los Angeles Times*, March 14, 2013, http://articles.latimes.com/2013/mar/14/business/la-fi-0315-wells-ceo-pay-20130315.

11. Carmen DeNavas-Walt and Bernadette D. Proctor, "Income and Poverty in the United States: 2013," *U.S. Census Bureau, Current Population Reports*, pp. 60–249 (Washington, DC: U.S. Government Printing Office, 2014), http://www.census.gov/content/dam/Census/library/publications/2014/demo/p60-249.pdf.

12. U.S. Department of Commerce, Bureau of Economic Analysis, "National Income and Product Accounts Tables," Table 6.16A, Corporate Profits by Industry, last revised August 7, 2013, http://www.bea.gov/iTable/iTable.cfm?ReqID=9&step=1#reqid=9&step=1&isuri=1&903=236.

13. *New York Stock Exchange Commission on Corporate Governance, Report of the New York Stock Exchange*

Commission on Corporate Governance, September 23, 2010, p. 12, http://www1.nyse.com/pdfs/CCGReport .pdf.

14. Ibid.

15. John C. Bogle, "Reflections on 'Toward Common Sense and Common Ground?,'" *The Journal of Corporation Law,* Vol. 33:1, p. 31.

16. Federal Reserve, *Financial Accounts of the United States* (Z.1), "Balance Sheet of Household and Non-profit Organizations," December 11, 2014, http://www .federalreserve.gov/releases/z1/current/z1r-5.pdf.

17. Data assembled for this book by the Bogle Financial Markets Research Center, comparison of US S&P 500 return (10.33%) and average equity fund investor return (6.48%), 1983–2011.

18. Investment Company Institute, "Characteristics of Mutual Fund Owners" (ch. 6), in *2014 Investment Company Fact Book,* accessed January 7, 2015, http:// www.icifactbook.org/fb_ch6.html#where.

Chapter 2—Sleepwalking into Retirement: The Shift from Pension to 401(k)

1. Employee Benefit and Research Institute website, "History of Pension Plans," March 1998, accessed January 7,

2015, http://www.ebri.org/publications/facts/index.cfm ?fa=0398afact.

2. Ibid.

3. Roger Lowenstein, "The End of Pensions," *New York Times*, October 20, 2005, http://www.nytimes.com/ 2005/10/30/magazine/30pensions.html?pagewanted= print&_r=0.

4. P. Purcell and J. Staman, *Summary of the Employee Retirement Income Security Act (ERISA)*, RS34443, Congressional Research Service, April 2008, http://dig italcommons.ilr.cornell.edu/key_workplace/505/.

5. Floyd Norris, "A Strategy for Pensions at Risk of Extinction," *New York Times*, December 4, 2014, http://www .nytimes.com/2014/12/05/business/without-new-laws -endangered-pensions-may-die.html.

6. Nathan Alderman, "What the Fool Is an IRA?," *Motley Fool*, June 3, 2010, http://www.fool.com/retirement/ iras/2010/06/03/what-the-fool-is-an-ira.aspx.

7. Laurence Arnold and Margaret Collins, "Edwin Johnson, 'Godfather' of 401(k) Retirement Plan, Dies at 82," August 30, 2012, *Bloomberg*, http//www.bloomberg.com/ news/2012-08-30/Edwin-johnson-godfather-of-401 -k-retirement-plan-dies-at-82.html.

8. Purcell and Staman, *Summary of ERISA*.

9. Ibid.

10. US Government Accountability Office, "2015 High Risk Report: Pension Benefit Guaranty Corporations Insurance Programs," http://www.gao.gov/highrisk/pension_benefit/why_did_study.

11. A.C.S., "Too Thin a Cushion," *Free Exchange* (blog), *Economist,* April 2, 2013, http://www.economist.com/blogs/freeexchange/2013/04/saving.

12. Anne Tergeson, "401(k) Law Suppresses Saving for Retirement," *Wall Street Journal,* July 7, 2011, http://online.wsj.com/news/articles/SB10001424052702303365804576430153643522780?mg=reno64-wsj&url=http%3A%2F%2Fonline.wsj.com%2Farticle%2FSB10001424052702303365804576430153643522780.html.

13. Jerry Geisel, "Fewer Employers Offering Defined Benefit Pension Plans to New Salaried Employees," October 3, 2012, *Workforce,* http://www.workforce.com/articles/fewer-employers-offering-defined-benefit-pension-plans-to-new-salaried-employees.

14. Elizabeth O'Brien, "10 Things 401(k) Plans Won't Tell You," February 23, 2013, *MarketWatch,* https://secure.marketwatch.com/story/10-things-401k-plans-wont-tell-you-2012-11-09.

15. Schwartz Center for Economic Policy Analysis, the New School, "Retirement Account Balances by Income: Even the Highest Earners Don't Have Enough," July 3, 2012, http://www.economicpolicyresearch.org/index .php/guaranteeing-retirement-income/528-retirement -account-balances-by-income-even-the-highest-earners -dont-have-enough-sp-1870142316.

16. Schwartz Center for Economic Policy Analysis, the New School, "Fact Sheet: SCEPA's Retirement Income Security Project," August 2013, http://www.econom icpolicyresearch.org/images/docs/SCEPA_blog/guar anteeing_retirement_income/Fact_Sheet_Retirement _Balances_july_2012_revised_FINAL.pdf.

17. AARP, Research and Strategic Analysis, *410(k) Partic-ipants' Awareness and Understanding of Fees*, Febru-ary 2011, http://assets.aarp.org/rgcenter/econ/401k-fees -awareness-11.pdf.

18. Christopher Carosa, "What Is An Appropriate Fee that a 401(k) Plan Should Pay?" August 6, 2013, *Fiduciary-News*, http://fiduciarynews.com/2013/08/what-is-an -appropriate-fee-that-a-401k-plan-should-pay.

19. Robert Powell, "9 Things You Need to Know About 401(k) Fees," July 8, 2014, *MarketWatch*, https://secure

.marketwatch.com/story/9-things-you-need-to-know
-about-401k-fees-2014-07-08.

20. Financial Industry Regulatory Authority website,
"Smart 401(k) Investing—Investing in Your 401(k),"
accessed January 7, 2015, http://www.finra.org/Inves
tors/SmartInvesting/Retirement/Smart401kInvesting/
investing/.

21. *Consumer Reports,* "How to Grow Your Savings: Stop
401(k) Fees from Cheating You Out of Retirement
Money," August 2013, http://consumerreports.org/cro/
magazine/2013/09/how-to-grow-your-savings/index.htm.

22. Fidelity.com, "Fees and Minimum Investments," in
"Compared Roth IRA vs. Traditional IRA," https://
www.fidelity.com/retirement-ira/ira/ira-comparison.

23. Fidelity Investments website, "Fidelity Money Market
Fund: Summary," accessed January 7, 2015, https://
fundresearch.fidelity.com/mutual-funds/summary/
31617H201.

24. Investment Company Institute, "Retirement Assets
Total $24.2 Trillion in Third Quarter 2014," December
17, 2014, http://www.ici.org/research/stats/retirement/
ret_14_q3.

Chapter 3—Who Watches While We Sleep?: From Watchdogs to Lapdogs

1. US Department of Justice website, "About DOJ," accessed January 7, 2015, http://www.justice.gov/about/about.html.

2. US Securities and Exchange Commission website, "The Investor's Advocate: How the SEC Protects Investors, Maintains Market Integrity, and Facilitates Capital Formation," accessed January 7, 2015, http://www.sec.gov/about/whatwedo.shtml#.UzLr-q1dV74.

3. US Commodity Futures Trading Commission website, "Mission & Responsibilities," accessed January 7, 2015, http://www.cftc.gov/About/MissionResponsibilities/index.htm.

4. Consumer Financial Protection Bureau website, "About Us," accessed January 7, 2015, http://www.consumerfinance.gov/the-bureau/.

5. US Senate Committee on Banking, Housing, and Urban Affairs, *Brief Summary of the Dodd-Frank Wall Street Reform and Consumer Protection Act*, July 1, 2010, http://www.banking.senate.gov/public/_files/070110_Dodd_Frank_Wall_Street_Reform_comprehensive_summary_Final.pdf; and H. R. 4173 (Dodd-Frank Wall Street Reform and Consumer Protection Act), 111th

Congress (2010), https://www.sec.gov/about/laws/wall streetreform-cpa.pdf.

6. Davis Polk, "3 Years of Dodd Frank," DavisPolk.com, July 2013, http://www.davispolkportal.com/info-graphic/july2013infographic.html.

7. Davis Polk, "Dodd-Frank Progress Report: December 1, 2014 Report," DavisPolk.com, December 2014, http://www.davispolk.com/Dodd-Frank-Rulemaking-Progress-Report/.

8. Jennifer Taub, "Taking Stock of Four Years of Dodd-Frank," *DealBook* (blog), *New York Times*, July 25, 2014, http://dealbook.nytimes.com/2014/07/25/taking-stock-of-four-years-of-dodd-frank/?_r=0.

9. Jim Spencer, "Does It Pay to Mix Politics, Business? Some Saying No," *Seattle Times*, March 3, 2013, http://seattletimes.com/text/2020467387.html.

10. Center for Responsive Politics/Open Secrets.org, "Influence & Lobbying: Ranked Sectors," accessed January 7, 2015, http://www.opensecrets.org/lobby/top.php?show Year=a&indexType=c; and "Finance/Insurance/Real Estate: Long-Term Contribution Trends," http://www.opensecrets.org/industries/totals.php?cycle=2012&ind=F.

11. Andrew Mayersohn, "Four Years After Citizens United: The Fallout," January 21, 2014, Center for Responsive

Politics/OpenSecrets.org, https://www.opensecrets .org/news/2014/01/four-years-after-citizens-united-the -fallout/.

12. Center for Responsive Politics/OpenSecrets.org, "Influence and Lobbying in the Securities & Investment Industry, 2014," accessed November 20, 2014, https:// www.opensecrets.org/lobby/indusclient.php?id=F07& year=2014.

13. US Department of the Treasury, *A New Foundation: Rebuilding Financial Supervision and Regulation*, 2009, p. 8, www.treasury.gov/initiatives/Documents/ FinalReport_web.pdf.

14. John C. Coffee Jr., *Gatekeepers: The Professions and Corporate Governance*, (Oxford, UK: Oxford University Press, 2006), p. 335.

15. Financial Industry Regulatory Authority website, "About FINRA," accessed January 7, 2015, http://www .finra.org/AboutFINRA/.

16. Mark Schoeff Jr., "Finra Calls Cease-Fire on RIA Oversight," *InvestmentNews*, February 7, 2013, http://www .investmentnews.com/article/20130207/FREE/ 130209953/finra-calls-cease-fire-on-ria-oversight.

17. Bruce Carton, "SEC to Receive 2% Budget Increase in FY 2014, Far Below 26% Requested Increase," *Compliance*

Week, January 2014, http://www.complianceweek.com/
blogs/enforcement-action/sec-to-receive-2-budget
-increase-in-fy-2014-far-below-26-requested-increase#
.VH9zSaTF-DA.

Chapter 4—Mutual Funds: The Big Sleep

1. Investment Company Institute, "Recent Mutual Fund
   Trends" (ch. 2), in *2014 Investment Company Fact Book*,
   accessed January 7, 2015, http://www.icifactbook.org/
   fb_ch2.html#assets.

2. Investment Company Institute, "Trends in Mutual Fund
   Investing, October 2014," http://www.ici.org/research/
   stats/trends/trends_10_14; and Federal Reserve, *Financial Accounts of the United States* (Z.1), "Balance Sheet
   of Household and Nonprofit Organizations," December
   11, 2014, http://www.federalreserve.gov/releases/z1/
   current/z1r-5.pdf.

3. Fidelity Investments website, "What Are Mutual Funds?,"
   accessed January 7, 2015, https://www.fidelity.com/
   learning-center/investment-products/mutual-funds/what-
   are-mutual-funds.

4. Fidelity, "What Are Mutual Funds?"

5. Investment Company Institute, "Trends in Mutual Fund
   Investing."

6. Elizabeth MacBride, "Fiduciary Standard Soon May Regulate Brokers-Dealers Deals," CNBC, April 29, 2013, http://www.cnbc.com/id/100662116.

7. US Securities and Exchange Commission website, "Plain Writing Initiative," accessed January 7, 2015, http://www.sec.gov/plainwriting.shtml.

8. US Securities and Exchange Commission website, "Form ADV," accessed January 7, 2015, http://www.sec.gov/answers/formadv.htm.

9. Fidelity.com, "Fidelity Magellan Fund," accessed December 7, 2014, https://fundresearch.fidelity.com/mutual-funds/summary/316184100.

10. Fidelity.com, "Fidelity by the Numbers: Corporate Statistics," accessed December 7, 2014, https://www.fidelity.com/about-fidelity/fidelity-by-numbers/corporate-statistics.

11. "The average adult reading speed for English prose text in the United States seems to be around 250 to 300 words per minute," Human Factors International, "Human Interaction Speeds," *User Interface Design Update*, August 2000, http://www.humanfactors.com/newsletters/human_interaction_speeds.asp.

12. Peter Lynch, *One Up on Wall Street: How to Use What*

You Already Know to Make Money in the Market, 2nd ed. (New York: Simon & Schuster, 2000).

13. Investment Company Institute, "Recent Mutual Fund Trends."

14. Fidelity, "What Are Mutual Funds?"

15. Sam Mamudi, "The Unseen Figures of Your Funds," *Wall Street Journal,* May 3, 2010, http://online.wsj.com/news/articles/SB100014240527487041006045751460 40314631942.

16. Ibid.

17. Interview with Jack Bogle, May 2012.

18. James Sterngold, "Is Your Fund's Board Watching Out for You?" *SmartMoney, Wall Street Journal,* June 9, 2012. http://online.wsj.com/articles/SB100014240527 02303753904577450243418998540.

19. Ibid.

20. Investment Company Institute, *2014 Investment Company Fact Book,* "Data Tables, Table 1," http://www .icifactbook.org/fb_data.html.

21. "Teresa Ghilarducci: Why the 401(k) Is a 'Failed Experiment,'" transcription of interview conducted for *Frontline,* "The Retirement Gamble," April 23, 2013, http:// www.pbs.org/ wgbh/ pages/ frontline/

business-economy-financial-crisis/retirement-gamble/ teresa-ghilarducci-why-the-401k-is-a-failed-experi ment/.

22. Charles Schwab, "'Highly Engaged' Americans Deeply Divided in Their Approach to Investing Says New Schwab Study," press release, June 12, 2013, http:// pressroom.aboutschwab.com/press-release/corporate -and-financial-news/highly-engaged-americans-deeply -divided-their-approach-in.

23. US Securities and Exchange Commission website, "Mutual Fund Classes," accessed January 7, 2015, http:// www.sec.gov/answers/mfclass.htm.

24. Investment Company Institute, "Frequently Asked Ques- tions About Mutual Fund Fee Disclosure," accessed January 7, 2015, http://www.ici.org/faqs/faq/faqs_fee _disclosure.

25. Investment Company Institute, "Trends in the Expenses and Fees of Mutual Funds, 2013," *ICI Research Perspec- tive*, May 2014, http://www.ici.org/pdf/per20-02.pdf.

26. Bogleheads.org, "Mutual Funds and Fees: The Effect of High Costs," accessed January 7, 2015, http://www .bogleheads.org/wiki/Mutual_funds_and_fees#The _effect_of_high_costs.

27. Investment Company Institute, "2014 Investment Company Fact Book," ICI Research Perspective, http://www.ici.org/pdf/2014_factbook.pdf.

28. James Sterngold, "Why Mutual Fund Guardians Are Failing," June 14, 2012, *MarketWatch*, https://secure .marketwatch.com/story/why-mutual-fund-guardians -are-failing-1339088682278. Note: averages have been calculated on an asset-weighted basis.

29. Russel Kinnel, "How Expense Ratios and Star Ratings Predict Success," *Morningstar*, August 9, 2010, http://news.morningstar.com/articlenet/article.aspx?id= 347327&t1=1322667532.

30. US Securities and Exchange Commission website, "Invest Wisely: An Introduction to Mutual Funds," accessed January 7, 2015, http://www.sec.gov/investor/pubs/inwsmf.htm.

31. US Department of Labor website, Employee Benefits Security Administration, "A Look at 401(k) Plan Fees," accessed January 7, 2015, http://www.dol.gov/ebsa/publications/401k_employee.html.

32. Data assembled for this book by the Bogle Financial Markets Research Center, comparison of US S&P 500 return (10.33%) and average equity fund investor return (6.48%), 1983–2011.

33. Investment Company Institute, "Characteristics of Mutual Fund Owners," (ch. 6), in "2014 Investment Company Fact Book," http://www.icifactbook.org/fb _ch6.html.

34. US Securities and Exchange Commission, 17 CFR Part 275, "Investment Adviser Performance Compensation," http://www.sec.gov/rules/final/2012/ia -3372.pdf.

35. US Securities and Exchange Commission website, "General Information on the Regulation of Investment Advisers," accessed January 7, 2015, http://www.sec .gov/divisions/investment/iaregulation/memoia.htm.

36. US Securities and Exchange Commission, "Investment Adviser Performance Compensation."

37. Casey Quinlan, "Should Managers Invest in Their Own Mutual Funds?" *U.S. News & World Report*, November 8, 2013, http://money.usnews.com/money/ personal-finance/mutual-funds/articles/2013/11/08/ should-managers-invest-in-their-own-mutual-funds? page=2.

38. Stephen Foley, "Why Investors Should Pick Managers with 'Skin in the Game,'" *Financial Times*, October 20, 2014, http://www.ft.com/cms/s/0/768b722c-582b-11e4 -a31b-00144feab7de.html#axzz3KfMaw1Mt.

39. Quinlan, "Should Managers Invest in Their Own Mutual Funds?"

40. James K. Glassman, "5 Mutual Funds for Socially Responsible Investors," *Kiplinger*, May 2012, http://www.kiplinger.com/article/investing/T041-C016-S001-5-mutual-funds-for-socially-responsible-investors.html.

41. AFL-CIO, "About the Mutual Fund Votes Survey," http://www.aflcio.org/Corporate-Watch/Paywatch-2014/Mutual-Funds-and-CEO-Pay/About-the-Mutual-Fund-Votes-Survey.

42. Joe Nocera, "C.E.O. Pay Goes Up, Up and Away!," *New York Times*, April 14, 2014, http://www.nytimes.com/2014/04/15/opinion/ceo-pay-goes-up-up-and-away.html?hp&rref=opinion.

43. *Equilar*, "Outlook on 2013 Say on Pay Responses," June 25, 2013, http://www.equilar.com/publications/articles/outlook-on-2013-say-on-pay-responses.

44. US Securities and Exchange Commission, "SEC Proposes Rules for Pay Ratio Disclosure," press release, September 18, 2013, http://www.sec.gov/News/PressRelease/Detail/PressRelease/1370539817895#.U0xo-7q1dXsk.

Chapter 5—No Escape from the Big Sleep

1. BarclayHedge, "Hedge Fund Industry—Assets Under Management," accessed December 1, 2014, http://www .barclayhedge.com/research/indices/ghs/mum/HF _Money_Under_Management.html.

2. Net worth excludes the value of a primary residence. An annual income of at least $200,000 will also qualify an individual as high net worth. US Securities and Exchange Commission website, "General Rules and Regulations, Securities Act of 1933," accessed January 8, 2015, https:// www.sec.gov/answers/accred.htm.

3. Lhabitant, *Handbook of Hedge Funds*, ch. 2.

4. Financial Industry Regulatory Authority website, "Fund of Hedge Funds—Higher Costs and Risks for Higher Potential Returns," accessed January 8, 2015, http:// www.finra.org/Investors/ProtectYourself/Investor Alerts/MutualFunds/p006028.

5. "Going Nowhere Fast," *Economist*, December 22, 2012, http:// www.economist.com/news/finance-and -economics/21568741-hedge-funds-have-had-another -lousy-year-cap-disappointing-decade-going.

6. Ryan McCarthy, "Counterparties: Sinking Alpha," Reuters, January 4, 2013, http://blogs.reuters.com/felix- salmon/2013/01/04/counterparties-sinking-alpha/.

7. Kelly Bit, "Hedge Funds Trail Stocks for Fifth Year with 7.4% Return," *Bloomberg*, January 8, 2014, http://www.bloomberg.com/news/2014-01-08/hedge-funds-trail-stocks-for-fifth-year-with-7-4-return.html.

8. Towers Watson, "The World's 300 Largest Pension Funds—Year End 2013," September 2014, http://www.towerswatson.com/en-US/Insights/IC-Types/Survey-Research-Results/2014/09/The-worlds-300-largest-pension-funds-year-end-2013.

9. Floyd Norris, "A Strategy for Pensions at Risk of Extinction," *New York Times*, December 4, 2014, http://www.nytimes.com/2014/12/05/business/without-new-laws-endangered-pensions-may-die.html.

10. Pension Benefit Guaranty Corporation website, "What Types of Plans Does PBGC Insure?" in "Your Guaranteed Pension," accessed January 8, 2015, http://www.pbgc.gov/wr/benefits/guaranteed-benefits/your-guaranteed-pension.html.

11. James B. Stewart, "Hedge Funds Lose Calpers, and More," *New York Times*, September 26, 2014, http://www.nytimes.com/2014/09/27/business/in-calperss-departure-a-watershed-moment-for-hedge-funds.html.

12. Josh Barro, "Calpers Isn't Done with High-Fee Investment Gurus," *The Upshot, New York Times*, October

2, 2014, http://www.nytimes.com/2014/10/03/upshot/ calpers-isnt-done-with-high-fee-investment-gurus .html?abt=0002&abg=0.

13. J.P. Morgan, *Capital Introduction Group: Institutional Investor Survey—2014*, 2014, https://www.jpmorgan .com/cm/BlobServer/is_survey_investorsinhedge funds.pdf?blobkey=id&blobwhere=1320639441026& blobheader=application/pdf&blobheadername1= Cache-Control&blobheadervalue1=private&blobcol= urldata&blobtable=MungoBlobs.

14. Fidelity.com, "Blackstone Alternative Multi-Manager Fund Class I," accessed January 8, 2015, https://fun dresearch.fidelity.com/mutual-funds/summary/ 09257V102.

Chapter 6—Awakened: A Better Way to Invest

1. MEMIC website, "Company Overview: History," accessed January 8, 2015, https://www.memic.com/ WHOWEARE/CompanyOverview/History/tabid/ 190/Default.aspx.

2. New Zealand Controller and Auditor-General, "Statements of Corporate Intent: Legislative Compliance and Performance Reporting," June 18, 2007, http://www .oag.govt.nz/2007/corporate-intent.

Chapter 7—Seven Ways to Reinvest

1. GIIRS Ratings & Analytics website, "What GIIRS Does," accessed January 8, 2015, http://www.giirs.org/about-giirs/about.

2. MSCI website, accessed March 11, 2015, http://www.msci.com.

3. Gimme Credit website, accessed January 19, 2015, http://www.gimmecredit.com.

INDEX